NORTHWEST GARDEN STYLE

NORTHWEST
GARDEN STYLE

NORTHWEST
GARDEN
STYLE

IDEAS, DESIGNS, AND METHODS
FOR THE CREATIVE GARDENER

JAN KOWALCZEWSKI WHITNER
PHOTOGRAPHS BY L. QUARTMAN YOUNKER

SASQUATCH BOOKS
SEATTLE

Published by Sasquatch Books.
Printed in Hong Kong.
Distributed in Canada by Raincoast Books Ltd.

Some material in this book appeared previously in the *Seattle Times* and in
Seattle Home and Garden magazine in similar or identical form. Material
on page 140 is from *Stonescaping,* by Jan Kowalczewski Whitner, 1992,
reprinted with permission of the publisher, Storey Communications,
Pownal, Vermont.

Credits:
Cover and interior photographs: L. Quartman Younker
Cover and interior design, graphics, and composition: Rohani Design,
Edmonds, Washington
Garden plans and diagrams: Jim Hays
Copy editor: Alice Copp Smith
Front cover photograph: David Lewis's and George Little's garden; back-
cover: Colleen and Kevin Stamper's garden; page iv: Stephanie and Larry
Feeney's garden; page viii: Pamela Georges's garden; page xii: Arthur
Erickson's garden.

Library of Congress Cataloging in Publication Data
Whitner, Jan Kowalczewski, 1949–
Northwest garden style : ideas, designs, and methods for the creative
gardener / Jan Kowalczewski Whitner : photographs by L. Quartman
Younker.
        p. cm.
    Includes index.
    1. Gardens—Northwest, Pacific. 2. Landscape gardening—
Northwest, Pacific. 3. Gardens—Northwest, Pacific—Design.
4. Gardens—Northwest, Pacific—Pictorial works. 5. Landscape
gardening—Northwest, Pacific—Pictorial works. 6. Gardens—
Northwest, Pacific—Design—Pictorial works. I. Title.
SB466.U65n7685 1996
712.609795—dc20   96-15293

Sasquatch Books
1008 Western Avenue
Seattle, Washington 98104
(206) 467-4300
books@sasquatchbooks.com
http://www.sasquatchbooks.com

Sasquatch Books publishes high-quality adult nonfiction and children's
books related to the Northwest (Alaska to San Francisco). For more information about our titles, contact us at the address above, or view our site
on the World Wide Web.

for
Shannon and Josh

Acknowledgments

Special thanks are due to Linda Younker, Stephanie and Larry Feeney, Margaret Willoughby, Richard L. Brown, Clare Hagen Dole, Jane Wentworth, Sadafumi Uchiyama, Arthur Kruckeberg, Bob Wiltermood, Hoichi Kurisu, and Florence and Paul Bliss. And to SW, for all his immoral support.

CONTENTS

PLANT LISTS

INTRODUCTION

GARDENING, LIKE POLITICS, is the art of the possible; in both fields, the most successful practitioners are flexible problem solvers who are able to maintain an ultimate vision, even as they encounter difficulties along the way.

In this sense, some of our best-designed gardens are simply creative solutions to specific landscaping problems.

Introducing a book on garden style by referring to problems and difficulties may seem a little dispiriting, but as any gardener knows, creating a garden plan that not only solves specific landscaping problems but also does it with a sense of style can seem like a daunting challenge at first.

Professional garden designers are trained to create landscapes that achieve proportion, balance, rhythm, and continuity—all those design components that, combined with a very personal spin, add up to "style"—in the course of dealing with practical site problems, such as eroding slopes or poorly draining soils. And in practicing their profession, these designers gradually learn many stylistically diverse ways to solve the same recurring practical problems.

But beginners (and often the most knowledgeable home gardeners still consider themselves beginners when it comes to questions of style) discover that invoking such abstract design concepts as scale, symmetry, and balance can seem useless when they are facing practical landscaping problems in the backyard. And because they usually aren't acquainted with hundreds of gardens that address the very problem they face in their own yards, beginners may not be aware of the variety of options they have.

This book is written to help nonprofessionals solve their landscaping problems by showing how other home gardeners have dealt with similar landscaping issues in their own backyards. Each of the chapters addresses a typical landscaping issue, and then demonstrates the various ways in which Pacific Northwest gardeners have responded to that issue. The gardens have been selected because they solve the problems practically, creatively, and with style.

Some garden design problems are universal in the sense that gardeners face them wherever they happen to garden. Creating visual flow between house and garden, planting for texture and color, creating year-round structure and interest—these challenges absorb gardeners from Toledo, Ohio, to Timbuktoo.

Many other design problems are specific to certain regions, dictated by special topographies, weather conditions, soil types, and water availability. Gardeners in both Alaska and the upper Midwest, for example, must choose from a relatively limited palette of plants that can withstand exceptionally harsh winter conditions, while seaside gardeners on either coast must use garden structures and plants impervious to high winds and salt spray.

In the maritime Pacific Northwest—which for purposes of this book extends on a north-south axis from Canada's lower British Columbia to Oregon's Willamette Valley, and on an east-west axis from the coastal mountain chains to the shores of the Pacific Ocean—gardeners deal with a mix of universal and region-specific design problems.

Physically, the area is characterized by cool, relatively dry summers and mild, wet winters; soils ranging in type from a poor glacial till scored into the ground by retreating glaciers ten thousand years ago, to hardpan clays and rich alluvial soils in river valleys; and a natural topography suitable for gardening that includes wooded hillsides rising over broad, flat valleys. The native plant palette, while not huge, contains some exceptionally ornamental varieties; and the climate allows regional gardeners to experiment with a very wide variety of plants, many of them imported from Europe, China, Japan, the Himalayan foothills of Southeast Asia, the Mediterranean basin, New Zealand, Asia Minor, and certain regions of Chile.

Historically, the Japanese and English landscaping styles have exercised a dominating influence on the region's gardens. Important strains within both of these traditions emphasize informal and naturalistic design, a style that is still very evident in today's Northwest garden. But as plants are introduced from the rest of the world, some of the design traditions associated with them—particularly Mediterranean garden styles—may come to play a more prominent role here.

As to Northwest gardeners themselves—the human factor in the gardening equation—they seem to display two fairly ubiquitous characteristics.

One is their love of the natural setting—their appreciation of the region as a unique landscape and environment, as well as their sense of its manifold gardening possibilities. Coupled with this sensibility is a very real desire to explore their own relationship with nature and to give, in the words of influential West Coast landscape architect Garrett Eckbo, "sensitive, esthetic expression in gardens . . . . to the very essence of the basic vitality of nature, that nature which is the world we live in, and which we are ourselves."

The second characteristic is a willingness to synthesize the styles and approaches of many of the world's different gardening traditions, and to adapt them to their own visions and requirements. Critics might refer to this eclectic style as derivative—as a pastiche of styles and traditions. One could dispute such an assessment by pointing out that mere imitation could never produce the graceful, self-confident, *working* designs found in private gardens throughout the Pacific Northwest, of which this book documents some notable examples.

This book differs from many other design-oriented gardening books in that, rather than discussing abstract design principles, it presents landscaping problems common to many Northwest gardens and then demonstrates a variety of ways that regional gardeners have solved them. The gardens profiled were chosen because they illustrate creative solutions for the most common Northwest gardening issues. I consulted a log of 10,000 inquiries directed to Seattle's Elisabeth Miller Horticultural Library by gardeners throughout the region, between 1989 and 1994, and from that log compiled a list of the most commonly asked landscaping questions. Although the questions were couched in terms that were sometimes practical, sometimes design-oriented, and sometimes a mix of the two, broad themes recurred. This book deals with the issues most frequently raised:

1. How do I plan and plant a natural garden, using Northwest native plants?

2. How do I plan and plant a wildlife-attracting garden?

3. How do I design and install hardscapes, such as paths, trellises, terraces, and fences?

4. How do I plan and plant a waterwise garden?

5. How do I plan and plant a small garden?

6. How do I plan and plant a water garden?

7. How do I plan and plant a garden on a slope?

8. Which are the best roses to add to my Northwest garden?

I would like to thank the many regional gardeners who graciously opened their gardens to Linda Younker and me in the course of our research. We discovered the gardeners as well as their gardens, and we experienced much fun, enlightenment, and comradeship during our visits. Some truly marvelous gardens that we visited do not appear in these pages only because they do not address the specific landscaping issues under discussion in the book.

1

NORTHWEST NATURAL GARDENS

THE PACIFIC NORTHWEST is well known for its snow-capped mountains, rugged coastline, and pristine waters. Gardeners all over the world also know it as the home of a small but choice selection of ornamental native plants.

English and Continental gardeners began adding Northwest natives to their landscapes early in the nineteenth century, after the British botanist-explorers Archibald Menzies and David Douglas traveled in our region collecting such attractive Northwest natives as Douglas firs *(Pseudotsuga menziesii)* and evergreen and deciduous huckleberries *(Vaccinium ovatum* and *V. parvifolium)*. In time, sword ferns *(Polystichum munitum)*, salal *(Gaultheria shallon)*, vancouveria *(Vancouveria hexandra)* and red-flowering currant *(Ribes sanguineum)* were added to the list of Northwest natives being planted in overseas gardens.

Curiously, early Northwest gardeners spent more time importing the kinds of plants found in East Coast and European gardens than exploring the ornamental potential of native plants growing in the forests surrounding them—perhaps because of the sentiment, common to pioneers in many regions, that natural landscapes are wildernesses to be subdued, not cherished.

By the turn of the twentieth century, Northwest gardeners were beginning to appreciate native plants, in part because of the influence of the Olmsted Brothers, the nation's foremost landscape architects, who between the 1890s and the 1930s designed the park systems for Portland, Seattle, Tacoma, and Spokane and well over a hundred private gardens throughout the region. Although the Olmsted Brothers were headquartered in Brookline, Massachusetts, they advocated using native vegetation in their designs for Northwest gardens, and they were especially alive to the beauty of the region's scenic views and natural landscape.

By the 1920s Japanese nurserymen and gardeners had also begun exerting an influence on Northwest garden design. Their tendency to use informal hardscapes and naturalistic plantings, with a preponderance of evergreen over deciduous material, especially suited the developing Northwest taste for natural-looking gardens. In the 1960s and 1970s, as development made inroads on the natural environment, gardeners were beginning to feel ecological as well as aesthetic imperatives for creating natural gardens. But enough of the Northwest landscape still remains intact today to provide regional gardeners with powerful inspiration and models when they attempt to express their perceptions of the landscape in a cultivated setting. With many regional nurseries propagating native plants, and with increasingly sophisticated techniques available for restoring natural landscapes or designing and maintaining naturalistic gardens, this type of gardening is becoming more popular than ever.

The natural landscape in the Pacific Northwest—which includes mountains, river valleys, and towering forests—is so massive in scale and so dramatic in impact that a gardener who wants to establish a natural-looking garden on a (usually) fairly circumscribed tract of land faces special practical and aesthetic challenges, among them:

- How to create the atmosphere or spirit of a natural landscape in a garden setting

- How to re-create authentic native plant associations and habitats on a small scale
- How to integrate hardscapes, functional garden spaces, and non-native plants into a natural-looking Northwest garden

✿ A SHAMAN'S RETREAT

John Braun's Garden
Whidbey Island, Washington

In a Northwest woodland, sunlight mottles trees and slides down moss-covered stumps to ferns and ground-covers that lie half-buried in the leafy debris of the forest floor. Visitors moving through the spongy duff brush by the branches of a flowering currant, setting its leaves quivering. A massive silence drenches the forest, quickly swallowing up the sounds of dead twigs snapping under boots, as well as a bird's faraway chatter. The grandeur and power of the natural landscape lie heavily on this tract of forest. So how does a gardener merge his or her own creative energy with what nature already has established here?

For John Braun, a retired architect who owns 5 acres of second-growth woodlands on the southern tip of Whidbey Island in Puget Sound, the answer lies in siting "natural" sculptures and other art installations in an otherwise minimally disturbed landscape. The heart and soul of John's forestland is a 1½-acre garden of natural, gently contoured hills and ravines covered by stands of hemlocks, Douglas firs,

A Shaman's Retreat

John Braun's Garden
Whidbey Island, Washington

GARDEN SITE	*A secluded wooded rural setting*
TOPOGRAPHY	*1½ acres of gentle hills and ravines, ringed by second-growth forest*
SOIL	*Acidic forest duff, amended in planted areas with composted horse manure*
LIGHT	*High shade with spots of filtered sunlight*
AVERAGE ANNUAL RAINFALL	*40 in.*
AVERAGE MINIMUM TEMPERATURE	*38° F (3.3° C)*
MAINTENANCE	*Sprinkler watering as needed; bouts of intense, contemplative maintenance*

huckleberries, and other native and exotic shrubs and groundcovers.

Within this garden space, John has set up "communities" of wood and stone objects that symbolize his relationship to the natural landscape, as well as the relationships he perceives among earth, water, rocks, and plants. By using the objects to concentrate, distill, and embody his ideas, John creates a "consecrated" atmosphere that can literally run chills up a visitor's back.

"This garden is where I attempt to bring magic into everyday life," says John. "It's a place where I can reveal, and express, and discover. Shamans are artists and magicians who are involved with transformation, with turning ignorance into knowledge, and chaos into order and meaning.

Above: An urn filled with "magic" willow twigs in John Braun's Whidbey Island, Washington, garden.

Opposite page: An altar dedicated to animal spirits in Braun's garden.

ORNAMENTAL NATIVE TREES FOR A NORTHWEST WOODLAND GARDEN

EVERGREEN CONIFERS

Abies procera	Noble fir	Handsome ridged bark and blue-green needles; grows slowly to 80 ft.
Chamaecyparis lawsoniana	Port Orford cedar (many cultivars)	Soft, droopy needles and many different habits, from shrubby to weeping. Some cultivars grow to only 5–6 ft.; the species grows to 50 ft. or more
Chamacyparis nootkatensis, C.n. 'Compacta' 'Pendula'	Yellow cedar	Conical shape, bluish needles; the cultivars grow to 10 ft., the species to 80 ft.
Juniperus scopulorum	Rocky Mountain juniper	Picturesque habit and blue-gray needles; does well in seaside gardens; 20–30 ft. in cultivation
Picea breweriana	Weeping spruce	Extremely tall but slow growing; elegant, like a mountain spruce in a Chinese scroll
Tsuga heterophylla	Western hemlock	Narrow tree to 100 ft. (*T. h.* 'Conica' is a dwarf) with glistening, soft green needles
Tsuga mertensiana	Mountain hemlock	Dull green needles on a densely branched trunk; 'Glauca' has bluish needles, 'Argentea' has needles with a silver cast

BROAD-LEAVED EVERGREENS

Lithocarpus densiflorus	Tan oak	Kruckeberg calls this an outstanding native plant for the garden but notes that it is seldom used. Leaves narrow, pointed, and heavily ribbed, trunk attractively curved; 20–30 ft.
Umbellularia californica	California bay laurel	Handsome shrub-tree with fragrant leaves; can tolerate some shade and drought; 5–80 ft., depending on conditions

DECIDUOUS TREES

Acer circinatum	Vine maple	Our Northwest counterpart to the Japanese maple, although the trunk can be multistemmed and the leaves are a little coarser; nice fall color; up to 25 ft. in prime conditions
Cornus nuttallii	Pacific dogwood	Stately tree to 40 ft. in gardens; lovely white flowers in spring and good fall foliage; fussy
Corylus cornuta californica	Western hazel	Dense, shrubby tree with character; thick, ribbed leaves, good fall color; to 15 ft.
Quercus garryana	Garry oak	Tall, aristocratic tree with a handsome, silvery trunk and spreading branches; thick, lobed leaves with acorn clusters; needs lots of space

ORNAMENTAL NATIVE SHRUBS FOR A NORTHWEST WOODLAND GARDEN

Amelanchier alnifolia	Serviceberry	Rounded 6- to 10-foot shrub with lovely white spring flowers and good fall color
Cornus stolonifera	Red-osier dogwood	White spring flowers, terrific fall foliage, clusters of berries in late summer; multiple-stemmed; quick-growing to 10 ft.; likes its feet wet
Garrya elliptica 'Issaquahensis'	Silk-tassel bush	Ev. shrub, 6–20 ft.; long, leathery leaves with silver undersides; catkins in winter make a nice display
Holodiscus discolor	Oceanspray	Spreading, rather coarse shrub to 15 ft. with gorgeous cloudy clusters of creamy white flowers in late spring; best used at the back of a shrub border
Leucothoe davisiae	Western leucothoe	Tropical-looking ev. shrub, slow-growing to 6 ft., with glossy hanging leaves
Myrica californica	Pacific wax myrtle	Fast-growing, open, ev. shrub with long, narrow, glossy leaves that grow compactly against the branch; to 10 ft.; protect from winter sun
Paxistima myrsinites	Oregon box	Dense ev. shrub good for groundcover situations; 3–4 ft.; attractive, shiny leaves
Philadelphus lewisii	Mock-orange	Vigorous vase-shaped shrub, 8–12 ft., with fragrant white flowers in midsummer
Rhododendron occidentale	Western azalea	Tall ev. shrub with attractive leaves and white/pink blooms in summer
Ribes sanguineum	Red-flowering currant	Open woodland shrub 6–10 ft. tall with lovely deep plum-pink flowers in spring
Vaccinium parvifolium	Deciduous huckleberry	Delicate sprays of tiny matte-green leaves and bright orangy red berries make this open 10-ft. shrub attractive in a woodland setting
Vaccinium ovatum	Evergreen huckleberry	Small, glossy leaves and small, purple-black fruits; usually shorter than its deciduous cousin, *V. parvifolium*

This garden has become a vehicle for changing myself, for transcending myself, too. It's the place where I learned how to be a shaman."

There are several entrances to the garden, each created to symbolize a different approach to, or relationship

Above: Spirit sculptures of wood, stone, and rubber strips stand guard near the shaman's entrance to Braun's garden.

Opposite page: Natural "totem poles," carved by the waters of Puget Sound, adorn a grove of trees.

between, nature and oneself. Today John takes us in the shaman's entrance, a narrow path almost obscured by tall shrubs, which means we have to stoop down—and, incidentally, view the landscape literally and metaphorically from a completely different perspective—in order to enter the garden.

Once in, we walk up a steep mound, on whose cleared crown stand 24 wooden objects—upended tree roots and large driftwood specimens—surrounded by low altars scattered with amulets, pottery masks, and votive candles.

"These wood sculptures have been worked on by natural forces for hundreds of years," says John. "Each one has a different story to tell of how it responds to pressure—the pressures of wind, the sun, water, and the earth. I imagine sounds coming from them, how they smell, how they would see, how they cast shadows behind them. . . . They remind me of how much I do not know about how the outside environment changes me, as well."

One wood sculpture stands to the side of the larger group, a representation of the link between the individual and the community. "I always place one individual piece near to but separate from my community pieces," John says, "because learning how to be an individual while remaining part of a group is one of the big tasks that everyone has to face during the course of their life."

Walking down from the mound along another narrow trail, we suddenly come into a clearing in the woods. Here about a dozen moss-covered stones, each one a landscape of colors, textures, and shapes in itself, lie half-buried in front of 13 wood "magicians"— stumps, roots, and limbs— each of which has been formed into an abnormal shape by a disease or fungus.

"These pieces of wood helped me to become a shaman, because while working with them I realized that human shamans are often lame, or albino, or somehow different from other people. But we have to honor what makes each of us different, because that difference is often the strongest part of each individual. Creating this garden is my way of expressing who I am—it helps me to create my own, personal myth."

Leaving the magicians' circle, we walk past another garden entrance, a narrow path almost engulfed by a large holly, its thousands of barbed leaves acting as a formidable barrier to anyone wanting to come through. Braun explains that this is his "prickly

ORNAMENTAL NATIVE GROUNDCOVERS AND HERBACEOUS PERENNIALS FOR A NORTHWEST WOODLAND GARDEN

Asarum caudatum	Wild ginger	Glossy, heart-shaped leaves on 8-in. stems
Berberis nervosa	Cascade oregon grape	Low-growing variety of Oregon grape (to about 2 ft.); attractive arching habit
Cornus canadensis	Bunchberry	Delightful groundcover about 6 in. high; nicely patterned leaves; neat white flower bracts in late spring, bright red fall berries
Fragaria spp.	Wild strawberry	Tough and vigorous; small leaves clustered along runners; many kinds have flowers and small fruits; *F. chiloensis* can take considerable drought once established
Gaultheria shallon	Salal	Leathery, rounded ev. leaves in mounds 1–4 ft. high; highly textured leaves nestle pleasingly around the base of Douglas firs in a woodland setting
Oxalis oregana	Wood sorrel (pink-flowering)	Cloverlike deciduous leaves; several inches tall; rather aggressive
Oxalis suksdorfii	Wood sorrel (yellow-flowering)	Similar to *O. oregana* but much easier to contain in a garden setting
Smilacena racemosa	False Solomon's seal	Long, narrow matte-green leaves cluster along an arching stem to 2½ ft.; creamy puffs of flowers in spring; a woodsy-looking plant with character
Tiarella trifoliata	Foam flower	Pretty, long-lasting white flower pokes up among attractive, ribbed leaves that stand several inches above the forest floor
Tolmiea menziesii	Piggy-back plant	Sheets of shaggy, heart-shaped leaves cover moist areas of the garden floor; a soothing background plant
Vancouveria spp.	Vancouveria	Neat, compact groundcovers that come in an evergreen and several deciduous types; likes moisture and semishade
Viola spp.	Woodland violet	A variety of these lovely little groundcovers will thrive in many different growing conditions, from poor, dry till to heavy, wet clay

In addition to the plants listed above, a large variety of native ferns and mosses are available at specialty nurseries and will add texture and shape to the woodland floor.

entrance," symbolizing how difficult access to self-knowl-edge and self-expression can be.

"Of course," he says, gesturing toward a cedar whose soft blue-gray branches droop across the other side of the path, "the same path can be easy to walk if you just follow it along a slightly different route."

In another clearing we encounter a community of wood sculptures adorned with crowns and necklaces of beads, feathers, and grasses that stands at the bottom of a shallow amphitheater. John says of this setting: "People have always created shrines in landscape settings where natural powers seem especially strong, where you can feel an unusual natural energy surging around. Well, art is powerful, and it triggers an exchange of energy between itself and whoever is viewing it."

Taking a stripped willow twig from a bundle of wood lying near the sculptures, Braun waves it like a magic wand across the entire garden, saying, "When I orchestrate the sounds and colors and shapes in this landscape, I become an artist. In making a whole garden, I become whole myself. In learning about the plants on this piece of land and how to nurture them, I become a healer."

Later, walking back with John to the garden entrance, the visitor mulls over how useful this incantation can prove to any gardener, as he or she begins the process of creating a personal garden space.

Asked what practical advice he would give to would-be natural gardeners, John says quickly and decisively, "First of all, don't start with a preconceived notion of what a garden ought to be. Then learn everything you can about the unique specifics of your site. Then think about the atmosphere you want to create in your garden. Finally, choose plants that will enhance your life, and whose lives you will enhance."

With those last thoughts, John Braun steps back through the shaman's entrance and disappears into his garden—like a magician vanishing into a sacred forest that is filled with mystery and meaning.

❧ RECIPE FOR A WETLAND
Robert Wiltermood's Garden
Port Orchard, Washington

Nationwide, well over 70 percent of our original native wetlands have been destroyed through development. Wetlands, which are defined most broadly as areas whose soils are saturated with water for significant portions of the year, play an important role in the ecosystem as catch basins for runoff surface water, as natural purifiers of standing water, and as habitat for native vegetation and wildlife.

In the Pacific Northwest their lush, hummocky pools and channels provide a healing and regenerative breeding ground for sedges, rushes, cattails, ducks, salamanders, fish, frogs, and dragonflies—all those watery life forms that, simmered together gently, make up the region's primordial soup.

Bob Wiltermood came by his love of wetlands early: he grew up on Ruby Creek Marsh, which became his family's home in 1923, when Bob's grandparents bought 80 acres of land and filled in part of the native wetlands in order to run cattle. When Bob and his brother Larry took over managing the family property in 1983, they decided to turn the cow pastures back to marshland, which would serve as a preserve for native plants and animals.

Larry, an engineer, and Bob, a wildlife specialist and wetlands conservationist, used a backhoe to dig ponds and channels in a 23-acre site, pulled out non-native vegetation that had crept into the site over the years, dammed up (with Department of Fisheries cooperation) nearby

Recipe for a Wetland	
Robert Wiltermood's Garden	
Port Orchard, Washington	
GARDEN SITE	*Small wetlands demonstration gardens set within a reclaimed marsh area*
TOPOGRAPHY	*Flat to gently sloping*
SOIL	*Water-saturated, acidic*
LIGHT	*High shade*
AVERAGE ANNUAL RAINFALL	*42 in.*
AVERAGE MINIMUM TEMPERATURE	*40° F (4.4° C)*
MAINTENANCE	*Minimal*

Above: Twenty-three-acre Ruby Creek Marsh in July, when ghostly snags—havens for insects and birds—rise above sheets of the rosy lavender blooms of native hardhack (Spiraea douglasii). *Below: Measuring approximately 8 feet on a side, this pocket-sized wetland is a fully functioning Northwest ecosystem.*

NORTHWEST NATIVE PLANTS FOR A SMALL WETLAND GARDEN

Carex spp.	Sedges	Clusters of grasslike spears; blades have squared-off edges; plant on water's edge
Eleocharis palustris	Spikerush	Stalks are narrow, spiky
Iris pseudacorus	Yellow iris	Pale yellow blooms in late spring; stately blades 3–5 ft. tall
Juncus spp.	Rushes	Grow in grasslike clusters at the edge of the water; 3–7 ft. tall
Lysichitum americanum	Skunk cabbage	Clumps of broad, glossy leaves; theatrical spring-flowering pale yellow bloom. Don't be deterred by common name—smells only when damaged
Mimulus guttatus	Monkey flower	Yellow monkey-face blooms add cheerful color to boggy areas that get sun
Nymphaea odorata	White water lily	Fragrant, 4-in. blooms hover over glossy, large pads; a tough beauty
Rorippa spp.	Watercresses	Tiny floating leaves prevent over-buildup of algae
Sagittaria latifolia	Wapato arrowhead	Arrow-shaped leaves poke above the water's surface for a tropical effect
Scirpus spp.	Bulrush	Leaf spears grow in clusters 3–10 ft. tall; can be invasive
Typha latifolia	Cattail	Stately blades grow 6–10 ft., topped by handsome brown seed heads

Ruby Creek to flood the area, and planted cattails, rushes, sedges, and other vegetation native to the area's natural wetlands. Bob and Larry established snags (dead, partially fallen tree trunks) in the marsh because almost half of the wildlife species that inhabit a wetland use snags at some point in their life cycles for feeding, hiding, or shelter.

Today ducks, horned owls, trumpeter swans, swallows, hawks, eagles, and other wildfowl use the wetlands, while chum salmon navigate the cattailed channels. School groups come through regularly to see how a wetlands ecosystem actually works, and photographers capture the teeming abundance of wildlife and native plants in their cameras' eyes. The Wiltermoods say the marsh will take

NORTHWEST NATIVE TREES, SHRUBS, AND VINES FOR PLANTING AROUND A WETLAND GARDEN

Cornus stolonifera	Red-osier dogwood	Medium-sized dec. shrub with white flowers, white or bluish berries, good fall color
Fraxinus latifolia	Oregon ash	Fast-growing dec. tree with compound leaves; extremely disease-resistant
Kalmia polifolia	Bog laurel	Small ev. shrub with attractive leaves
Lonicera involucrata	Black twinberry	Vine with orange blooms attractive to bees, butterflies, and hummingbirds; thread it through a shrub for extra color and texture
Populus tremuloides	Quaking aspen	Small, delicate tree with leaves that flutter beautifully in the wind; glorious fall color
Physocarpus capitatus	Pacific ninebark	Attractively layered bark and white spring flowers; likes high shade
Rubus parviflorus	Thimbleberry	Tall dec. shrub with white flowers in spring and red berries in midsummer
Rubus spectabilis	Salmonberry	Medium-sized dec. shrub with pinkish flowers and bright red fruits
Salix spp.	Willow	Shrubby dec. trees with graceful leaves
Spiraea douglasii	Hardhack	Coarse, dense dec. shrub with attractive rosy-lavender blooms from late spring through July

almost two hundred years to once again approach a truly natural state, and they are making plans to ensure that Ruby Creek Marsh will remain undisturbed for many generations to come.

Because Bob believes that more Northwesterners should be able to enjoy a wetlands environment wherever they live, he has been experimenting with creating small wetlands habitats—habitats big enough to contain a functioning ecosystem, but small enough to fit into a constricted urban lot. Bob's company designs and installs wetlands areas for public spaces and private gardens, but he believes that the average home gardener can create his or her own wetlands, using easily available tools and vegetation bought from regional nurseries specializing in native wetlands plants.

It is relatively easy to create a wetland in a crowded urban setting, since even a garden space little more than a few square feet in size can support a functioning habitat. Here, according to Bob's recipe, is how you can transform any garden space into a whole new—and natural—world:

1. Dig an irregular depression about 2 feet deep, in the shape of the wetland you want to establish.
2. Enlarge the depression by creating a shallow shelf about 1 foot wide and 1 foot deep around the perimeter of the hole.
3. Line the hole with plastic, leaving enough plastic to reach up to and cover the shallow shelf.

Above: The aesthetics of decay: a natural collage of sunlight, stone, moss, and wood.

Opposite page: Lush stands of alders, Douglas firs, devil's club (Oplopanax horridum), *ferns, and reeds create Bob Wiltermood's Northwest wetlands garden.*

4. Anchor the plastic to the edge by covering it with soil and/or rocks.

5. Fill in the hole with approximately 18 inches of the original soil, amended with peat moss, or with a good grade of new topsoil.

6. Plant the depression with native wetland plants, using a plank or ladder laid across the soil-covered surface to reach the center.

7. Slowly seep water into the depression up to the level of the surface; rainwater or untreated water is best, but tap water can be used.

8. Let the new environment settle in for several days before introducing aquatic wildlife.

Once your wetland is planted, it will gradually establish its own balance—further maintenance, other than topping off the water level occasionally, is seldom required. The submerged and emergent vegetation, such as rushes, sedges, and cattails, will keep the water oxygenated and clean, and the fish, birds, and other wildlife will feed on the tiny crustaceans and insects that have been carried in by wind, by the feet and feathers of previous visiting wildlife, or by artificial transplant.

Bob stresses the importance of placing "large organic debris"—such as standing and submerged snags—in your new wetland. Snags protect and feed wildlife, and slowly add nutrients to the habitat as they rot.

On a design note, Bob suggests that for both practical and aesthetic reasons a boardwalk, rather than a turf lawn, is the best hardscape to place around a created wetland. A boardwalk is much easier to maintain than a lawn and doesn't require the use of fertilizers and herbicides that could accidentally leach into the wetland. A boardwalk can neatly cover the edges of the wet areas, which are sometimes difficult to make pleasing to the eye, and it permits visitors to feel immediately in touch with the wetland, as though they were skimming over its surface at close range.

❧ "BLURRING THE EDGES" BETWEEN THE WILD AND THE CULTIVATED

John Kenyon's Garden
Redmond, Washington

"It sounds paradoxical to say it like this—but it's very complex to design a natural garden," says landscape architect John Kenyon, whose own woodland garden features stands of conifers, rhododendrons, and vine maples fringing a rock-strewn pond half-smothered in groundcovers, ferns, and mosses.

John's garden looks like an especially lovely slice of the natural landscape—and it possesses the simplicity, restfulness, and seclusion that he believes are the qualities people especially value in natural sites.

But the berm on which the carefully chosen and artfully sited trees and shrubs are planted was mounded there less than eight years ago by a backhoe, which also scooped out the pond and tumbled the rocks into place around its rim. Even the stream flowing down the slope channels runoff surface water from a housing development farther up the hill.

"A natural garden is actually a completely contrived symbol of nature," John contends, "and the real challenge to designing one is making it feel uncontrived—to make it feel real, not kitschy."

Kenyon believes that one of the most difficult challenges in creating a

---

"Blurring the Edges" Between the Wild and the Cultivated

John Kenyon's Garden
Redmond, Washington

GARDEN SITE	*A natural garden set within a larger rural property*
TOPOGRAPHY	*Sheltered, artificially contoured slope approximately 100 ft. wide by 50 ft. deep facing southwest*
SOIL	*Acid, composed of glacial till covered by a layer of humus*
LIGHT	*High shade with a maximum of two hours of filtered sun*
AVERAGE ANNUAL RAINFALL	*40 in.*
AVERAGE MINIMUM TEMPERATURE	*Mid-30s F (around 1.7° C); there is a cold pocket surrounding the stream where plants that are hardy in the rest of the garden may die off in a cold winter*
MAINTENANCE	*Medium*

Above: A complementary mix of Northwest native and exotic plants in John Kenyon's Redmond, Washington, garden.

Opposite page: A beautifully designed stream carries excess runoff from a housing development located several miles upstream from Kenyon's garden.

Northwest natural garden lies in establishing a comfortable relationship of scale between the vast natural landscape and a single garden setting.

"Of course, if you have a reasonably big space to play with, then it's easier to do," he says, using his own garden as an example.

It's sited on a wooded slope tucked into a second-growth hillside, and John planted tall-growing western red cedars and Leyland cypresses along the high edge of the property to act as a quick-growing visual boundary that blends into the adjacent natural landscape. A hemlock was planted in front of the cedars and cypresses so that its lacy, blue-tinged foliage would show up against their furrowed cinnamon bark. Closer in the foreground stands a *Euonymus alatus,* a non-native, woodsy-looking shrub whose leaves turn a splendidly rich burgundy in autumn. (*E. alatus* has a Northwest native cousin, *E. occidentalis,* that purists might want to plant instead, but the native is far inferior in habit and color.)

EXOTIC PLANTS THAT COMPLEMENT A WOODLAND GARDEN

EVERGREEN TREES AND SHRUBS

Aucuba japonica		Ev. shrub, 8–10 ft. with glossy leaves; a tranquil mingler
Camellia spp.		Ev. shrubs and climbers; varieties with single flowers suit the quiet native atmosphere better than the fussy-looking doubles; plant Sasanqua varieties for winter and early spring bloom
Chamaecyparis spp.		Tall ev. shrubs and trees that mingle well with native conifers
Cryptomeria japonica	Japanese cryptomeria	Tall ev. tree with soft, textured needles; most cultivars are much smaller, shrubby
Daphne odora	Winter daphne	Ev. shrub, slow-growing 6–8 ft., with very fragrant winter flowers; needs protection from cold
Kalmia latifolia	Mountain laurel	Medium-sized ev. shrub with neat, shiny leaves; pink flowers in midspring
Leucothoe fontanesiana	Drooping leucothoe	Ev. shrub, slow-growing to 8 ft. with glossy leaves; a quiet "structure" plant with an informal habit
Loropetalum chinensis		Slow-growing ev. shrub to 5–6 ft.; small, lovely oval leaves with dusty green and purple tinges; pretty flowers in spring that recur in summer and fall; very tender in Seattle gardens and north, but well worth the effort
Pinus thunbergiana	Japanese black pine	Characterful pine growing 30 ft. and up, with flaky bark and attractively gnarling trunk
Rhododendron Loderi hybrids		Rhodies growing 6–8 ft., with unusually handsome leaves and blooms
Rhododendron yakushimanum		Smaller, especially hardy rhodies with a compact form that complements many Northwest native groundcovers
Sarcococca hookerana humilis, S. ruscifolia		Spreading ev. shrubs with glossy leaves and wonderfully fragrant winter flowers. *S. h. humilis* is a low groundcover, *S. ruscifolia* grows slowly to about 5 ft.
Stranvaesia davidiana		Tall ev. shrub-tree that serves as an informal structural plant for backgrounds

EXOTIC PLANTS THAT COMPLEMENT A WOODLAND GARDEN (cont.)

DECIDUOUS TREES AND SHRUBS

Acer palmatum, *A. japonica*	Japanese maples	Many varieties, sizes, habits, and foliage colors
Amelanchier spp.	Serviceberry	Graceful shrubs and trees 6–25 ft. tall, with attractive leaves and white flowers in spring
Cercidiphyllum japonicum	Katsura tree	Elegant tree with neat branching patterns, to 40 ft.; handsome, fluttering leaves have a remarkable fragrance; brilliant color in fall
Cornus florida	Flowering dogwood	Small, neat tree with dense branches and beautiful spring blooms; look for new disease-resistant varieties
Cornus kousa		Shrubby tree to 16 ft.; nice fall color
Corylopsis pauciflora	Fragrant winter hazel	Small tree with pale, deliciously scented winter flowers
Enkianthus campanulatus		Neat, tiered branches hold leaves that turn scarlet in fall; 8–15 ft.
Hamamelis spp.	Witch hazel	Compact trees with attractive trunks and fragrant winter flowers; usually under 12 ft.
Rosa rugosa		Tough, drought-tolerant species roses to 6 ft. tall, usually with single pink or white blooms
Sambucus spp.	Elderberry	Tall shrubs with droopy, tropical-looking paired leaves; need lots of room for their open, ragged habit
Stewartia spp.		Handsome trees with attractive bark, trunks, and summer flowers; complement rhododendrons especially well

The following well-known perennials, bulbs, and groundcovers will also complement a Northwest native planting: anemones, bergenia, crocuses, hardy cyclamen, *Digitalis, Epimedium,* heucheras, hostas, scillas, primulas, violas, and vincas.

Such natives as serviceberry, elderberries (especially variegated-leaf types), red-osier dogwoods, and flowering currants also could be tucked into the same foreground area. John suggests interplanting them with compatible exotic shrubs, such as the yakushimanum rhododendrons, in order to extend the available plant palette.

Ferns and native groundcovers, such as Oxalis oregana *and* O. suksdorfii, *help create a richly textured garden floor.*

This overstory of trees and shrubs creates a rich tapestry of textures and colors. It also acts as a mediating buffer between the larger natural landscape farther up the slope and the smaller, more intimately scaled garden room that has been established lower down, near the pond and stream.

Kenyon used Loderi hybrid rhododendrons to encircle and define the pond room: he thinks their form, foliage, and blooms are superior to those of our native rhododendron *(Rhododendron pacificum),* while having enough visual associations with Northwest native shrubs to look in place in a natural setting. Underneath the rhododendrons, native groundcovers such as kinnikinnick *(Arctostaphylos uva-ursi)* and wintergreen *(Gaultheria procumbens)* scramble among ferns, mosses, and low-growing exotics that also have a Northwest, woodsy feel to them, including hostas and Taiwan rose *(Rubus calycinoides).*

The woodland and pond gardens feature informal Japanese hardscapes and ornaments—stepping-stone paths, a rustic teahouse, rough stone lanterns—because Kenyon feels they blend quite seamlessly into a natural-looking garden.

John had the space to create a comfortable flow between the scale of his garden and the scale of the natural landscape. But what if your lot is small, yet you still yearn to create a natural garden that looks "right" in the larger context?

In such a case, John suggests, adopt the basic Japanese gardening principle of "borrowing" trees and other

Kenyon's garden features low-key, rustic-looking hardscapes with a Japanese touch, a style he recommends for Northwest natural gardens.

prominent plants outside your garden's boundaries to establish its background scale. The plants inside your garden then become the foreground to this taller back-drop. Such an approach leaves you enough room to create a rich and dense foreground, filled with plenty of interesting varieties of shrubs and groundcovers.

Hardscapes and natural screens play a crucial role in the small natural garden, providing it with privacy from neighbors and blocking out unsightly views. You can estab-lish low-key, natural-looking garden boundaries by using stands of bamboo or easily pruned Leyland cypresses. If your space is too small to accommodate such hedges, fences made from such roughly finished materials as grape stakes or split bamboo will perform the same functions in less space.

Because it is necessary to firmly and dramatically intro-duce a reduced scale into a small natural garden, John sug-gests you follow another classic Japanese design principle:

bring the essence of a natural feature or a natural landscape into a garden setting, miniaturize its essential elements and then place it in sharp relief against one or two other carefully selected miniaturized natural elements. In this way you can attempt to symbolize all of nature in a few carefully designed and executed square feet of garden space. Several rocks and a berm can evoke whole mountains; a small trickle of water winding through moss can represent a stream or river; and a rumpled blanket of groundcovers can symbolize a forest.

The point here is not to literally replicate natural landscapes on a miniature scale—if so, can model trains and their tracks be far behind?—but to capture the essence of a natural feature and place it in your garden on a reduced scale. Juxtaposing several of these features will underline their essential characters even more profoundly: the quicksilver nature of water's movement becomes especially apparent when it flows through a small channel of immovable stones.

Envisioning these symbolic features is a complex task that draws on the gardener's sense of physical, spiritual, and aesthetic connection to nature. It's a connection that many regional gardeners want to explore on all three levels. As John Kenyon says, "When we create a landscape, we are expressing our values. And even as nature is beginning to slip away from us more and more in our daily lives, we are coming to realize that we need a kind of healing that only the natural landscape can provide."

CHECKLIST FOR CREATING A NORTHWEST NATURAL GARDEN

- Observe precisely where native plants grow in their natural habitats, and try to establish them in similar growing conditions in your garden. For instance, shrubs or groundcovers that seem to thrive on a dry, sunny bank in a woodland glade will probably do well on a similar bank in your garden, while plants that live along the shady, moist banks of a stream at the bottom of a ravine will need the same cool, wet growing conditions in the backyard.

• Look at natural associations of native plants to get ideas for how to interplant natives in your garden. For instance, western hemlock *(Tsuga heterophylla)*, sword ferns *(Polystichum munitum)*, evergreen and deciduous huckleberries *(Vaccinium ovatum* and *V. parvifolium)*, and salal *(Gaultheria shallon)* can combine naturally for a harmonious blending of colors, textures, and shapes. Consider interplanting compatible exotics among your native plants in order to extend the available palette.

• If a tree grows in high country in the wild, plant it in a high spot in the garden; if a plant grows wild in a meadow, try to grow it in an open, flat, sunny spot in the garden. This is important not only to replicate growing conditions but in order to set each plant in its appropriate design environment. For instance, a tough, gnarled, windsculpted "mountain" pine will look in place on a rocky ledge near the top of a berm, but out of place in a low, protected marsh, surrounded by lush swaths of iris and cattails.

• Use informal hardscapes that blend well into a natural setting. For paths, use wood chips rather than cut flagstones; for fences, use rough grape stakes instead of mortared bricks; for a bench, use a plank balanced on rocks instead of a wrought-iron love seat.

• Use native groundcovers in place of turf lawns wherever possible.

• If you garden in a small space, consider using the more dainty cultivars of large Northwest natives—such specimens retain the look, but not the towering size, of the species plants.

• Leave rotting stumps, fallen tree trunks, and other signs of nature's life cycle in the garden.

• When you plant an entire natural garden landscape, establish the layers that are found in your typical natural landscape. In most of the Northwest, this typical layering consists of an overstory or canopy of trees; tall shrubs; smaller shrubs and herbaceous perennials; and groundcovers, mosses, and lichens.

A Parting Thought: Why Not Moss?

Given that moss thrives in the acidic soils, shady exposures, and humid climate of much of the Pacific Northwest, it seems counterproductive that many regional gardeners spend time and energy trying to eradicate it from the home landscape.

You can use the strong decorative qualities of moss in your natural garden in the following ways:

- Let a tapestry of mosses and lichens cover stumps and raised ground roots, instead of removing these natural features.
- Let mosses visually tie together features made of different materials—a moss carpet covering a rock and a prone tree trunk lying at a pool's edge bring magic to a woodland garden scene.
- Consider creating a moss lawn, instead of a turf lawn, in any shady stretch. Moss lawns are evergreen, and need no mowing or fertilizing. Just be sure to weed regularly and to rake the moss lawn often, to keep fallen garden debris from smothering it.

Here are three methods for introducing moss into your garden:

- Spread cheesecloth over a flat of good garden soil, spread small quantities of moss mixed with sugar and water over the cloth's surface, and keep the flats moist and shaded for six weeks. Once the moss has covered the cloth, cut up strips and transplant them to your garden.
- Grind up moss-covered portions of rotting Douglas firs and cedars, then introduce the mixture to shady, moist spots in your garden.
- Mix dried-up crumbled moss with buttermilk or beer, and pour the mixture over stones or tree trunks; keep the area moist and shaded.

Opposite page: Time-worn statuettes nestle at the base of a towering evergreen, both elements evoking a sense of age, in a corner of John Kenyon's garden.

2

GARDENS FOR ATTRACTING WILDLIFE

THE MOST DELIGHTFUL TASK that God gave to Adam when he lived in the Garden of Eden was naming "every beast of the field and every bird of the air." Ever since, Paradise has been known as the place where the lions lie down with the lambs—a sanctuary for animals ruled and protected by an Adam and Eve still in their original state of grace. This tradition of associating animals and paradisiacal landscapes continues in Western gardening throughout history.

Early Egyptians brought in ibises and other tamed waterfowl to splash in their lily-filled pools, Romans displayed nightingales in ornate garden aviaries, and Charlemagne kept bears and deer—as well as an elephant!—at his palace grounds in Aix-la-Chapelle. Later, the great formal gardens of England and the Continent often featured aviaries, fishponds, and even deer parks.

Other world cultures also associate garden-paradises with habitats for animals. Ancient Chinese emperors brought wild beasts from exotic corners of their domain to their imperial gardens, and Aztec kings filled their pleasure gardens with rare birds, fish, and reptiles.

Pacific Northwesterners love to populate their gardens with wildlife too, but the modern regional taste tends less toward capturing and displaying rare and exotic beasts and more toward inviting our native Northwest fauna to come in and make themselves at home.

In the process of creating such landscapes, gardeners naturally begin to learn about the life cycles and habitat requirements of birds, butterflies, fish, bats, toads, bees, salamanders, and other native wild creatures. Thus landscaping for wildlife helps Northwestern gardeners widen an appreciation of the natural world around us that perhaps starts with a love of plants but then almost inevitably grows richer and more complex.

This appreciation begins in subtle ways. It can happen one day while you are watching the image of a cattail glimmer in still water and then suddenly notice the tadpoles wiggling around its muddy roots. Your gaze slides up the cattail's stalk, shuddering now under the furious attack of a marsh wren, who batters the tough brown seed heads until they burst apart. A blue heron dozes nearby, perched on one leg. Hearing the slow, hollow plunk of a frog slipping into water, the heron stretches his neck and opens a single golden eye, its black pupil as sharp and cold as obsidian. Such moments can move those who observe them in ways too subliminal to understand, and heal them in ways too delicate to assess.

Despite the massive global destruction wrought on wildlife habitat during the last half century, a great chain of being still wraps around the natural world, and its fragile links are fish, birds, insects, toads, and other living creatures. Gardeners can help preserve this chain by nurturing their gardens and the wildlife they attract. This chapter presents gardeners who have rehabilitated disturbed landscapes to attract birds, salmon, and trout. It also suggests how to create garden environments that will nurture and sustain a host of other regional native species.

❧ BIRD-SCAPING THE BACKYARD
Rosemarie Stefanich's/Peggy Church's Garden
Redmond, Washington

When Peggy Church bought a house in a newly developed community atop the Sammamish Plateau east of Seattle in 1987, bulldozers had stripped the surrounding landscape of all vegetation other than several bigleaf maples and western red cedars. (The maples and cedars, their roots irreparably damaged by soil compacted by the heavy construction equipment, are now slowly dying—the lingering mementos of a vanished landscape.) The tangled undergrowth that naturally prevents erosion and drainage problems on undisturbed terrain had also been skinned off the hillside. As a result, Peggy and her neighbors confronted new back-yards filled with barren subsoils and large mudholes.

Peggy, a dedicated bird-watcher, decided to create an attractive, bird-friendly environment in her new garden. As she studied lists of plants that provide birds with shelter, food, and nesting, she realized that planting Northwest natives could play a crucial role, not only in providing habitat for birds, but also in solving her backyard's erosion and drainage problems.

Her small garden sits on a narrow sloping lot that wraps around the back of the house in a series of sharply angled "outdoor rooms," with the outside perimeters backing up on neighbors' fences. With the assistance of Seattle garden designer Greg McKinnon,

Bird-Scaping the Backyard
Rosemarie Stefanich's/Peggy Church's Garden
Redmond, Washington

GARDEN SITE	*Suburban development*
TOPOGRAPHY	*A sheltered, forested slope with a western exposure*
SOIL	*Hard clay, with some amended planting areas*
LIGHT	*Variable throughout the day, with all garden areas receiving sun for a minimum of two hours*
AVERAGE ANNUAL RAINFALL	*40 in.*
AVERAGE MINIMUM TEMPERATURE	*38° F (3.3° C); some high winds in January and February rake across the garden, effectively lowering the minimum temperature*
MAINTENANCE	*Low, except in autumn, when leaves, seeds, and other garden debris are collected and removed*

Peggy created several different zones of natural plantings in this initially unpromising space.

An installed stream with a recirculating pump provides fresh, moving water for birds to drink and bathe in.

Between the house and one fence line they planted a small grove of native conifers, including grand fir, Douglas fir, blue Engelmann spruce, shore pine, and western hemlock. Moss-covered snags left over from the original forest landscape lie half-buried in the ground, serving as forage and protection for insects and birds. Over the years, as the

NORTHWEST NATIVE PLANTS FOR ATTRACTING BIRDS

Amelanchier alnifolia	Serviceberry	Dec. shrub 6–10 ft.; small, dark fruits in late summer
Aquilegia spp.	Columbine	Dainty spring flowers provide nectar
Arbutus menziesii	Madrone	Large, broad-leaved ev. tree with peeling bark; orange-red fruits in fall, winter
Arctostaphylos uva-ursi	Kinnikinnick	Ev. groundcover; berries in fall, winter
Ceanothus spp.		Ev. shrubs and groundcovers; berries
Cornus nuttallii	Western dogwood	Large dec. tree; red fruits attract cedar waxwings, American robins, downy woodpeckers
Cornus stolonifera [*C. sericea*]	Red-osier dogwood	Large dec. shrub; likes moist habitat; white or bluish fruits
Gaultheria shallon	Salal	Ev. groundcover; black fruits
Holodiscus discolor	Oceanspray	Medium-sized dec. shrub; white summer flowers attract birds
Mahonia spp.		Ev. shrubs and groundcovers; blue-black fruits
Myrica californica	Pacific wax myrtle	Large ev. shrub; long-lasting purple berries
Oemleria cerasiformis [*Osmaronia cerasiformis*]	Indian plum	Large dec. shrub: summer fruit
Ribes sanguineum	Flowering currant	Med.-sized dec. shrub: blue-black berries
Sambucus spp.	Elderberry	Large dec. shrub; late-season fruits
Symphoricarpos albus	Snowberry	Med.-sized dec. shrub; white fall berries
Vaccinium parvifolium	Red huckleberry	Large dec. shrub; bright salmon-red fruits through summer attract grouse, American robin, common flicker

*Plants that are especially attractive to hummingbirds

conifers mature, they will create cover and nesting spots for birds, a source of compost for groundcovers, and shade, privacy, and enclosure for people.

Attractive native shrubs such as flowering currant, red elderberry, Indian plum, and oceanspray were planted in a semisunny area near the evergreen stand to provide seasonal seeds and fruits for birds. The roots of the shrubs have helped stabilize the garden's sloping terrain, and the leaves, seeds, fruits, and bark they drop regularly are slowly establishing a rich humus to support a variety of decorative native groundcovers and ferns that are planted in the shade at their feet.

Near the shrubbery, Church and McKinnon installed a lined pond with a circulating pump. The pond has shallow wading areas filled with small stones where birds can perch to bathe and drink; it also has a small island in its center where they can safely roost. A stream, bordered by salal, wild ginger, and patches of native columbine, wanders between this pond and several smaller ones farther down the slope, which act as spillover basins for surface water by funneling excess runoff into a dry streambed of gravel and drain rock. Native sedges and red-osier dogwoods dot the dry streambed, and the handsome red branches of the dogwood add color to the garden in winter.

In an open spot near the house that receives sun most of the day, a patch of strawberries and blueberry bushes provides fruits for birds and humans alike—no nets, whirligigs, or scarecrows have ever been used to prevent the birds from getting their share of the harvest here.

Nowadays the garden is quiet, green, and secluded, like a little bit of forest left to slumber in the heart of a compact, bustling neighborhood. Its present owner, Rosemarie Stefanich, says that when she eats lunch on her back deck she feels as though she's picnicking in a woods. The yard is a constant source of wonder to her, reminding her of what it felt like to play—maybe even get a little lost!—when she visited the forest as a child.

And neighbors up and down the street seem to feel that enchantment too. Several gardens featuring bird-attracting plants, naturalistic planting schemes, and ponds have sprung up in the development, all of them playing a part in healing this particular slice of landscape and, in the process, welcoming the birds back to their original habitat. (See the checklist at the end of this chapter for additional bird-attracting landscaping ideas.)

HUMMINGBIRDS—JEWELED DARTS IN THE GARDEN

By mid-February, five types of hummingbirds—rufous, blackchinned, Allen's, Calliope, and Anna's species—are beginning to arrive in the Pacific Northwest from their Mexican wintering grounds. The males—brightly plumaged and pugnaciously territorial—show up first, followed shortly by the more soberly colored females, who establish tiny nests, lay precisely two eggs, and then become busy feeding the babies once they hatch. After midsummer most hummingbirds leave our gardens for points farther north.

Opposite top: A rufous hummingbird finds a resting spot in Rosemarie Stefanich's garden.

Opposite below: Stefanich's small, sharply angled suburban lot is a carefully designed haven for birds.

PLANTS FOR ATTRACTING HUMMINGBIRDS

Ajuga spp.	Bugleweed	Dec. groundcover; blue flowers in May
Begonia spp.	Begonia	Summer-long flowers
Buddleia davidii	Butterfly bush	Large dec. shrub; blue, purple, white, or lavender flowers in summer
Dicentra spp.	Bleeding heart	Perennial with delicate spring flowers
Digitalis spp.	Foxglove	Tall biennials with spikes of tubular flowers
Echinacea purpurea	Purple coneflower	Perennial with purple, white summer flowers
Fuchsia spp.	Fuchsia	Summer-long ruffled blooms
Heuchera spp.	Coral bells	Low perennial with handsome leaves, spring flowers
Lilium spp.	Lilies	Tall plant with fragrant summer flowers
Lonicera spp.	Honeysuckle	Dec. vine with fragrant summer blooms
Monarda didyma	Bee balm	Perennial with stately summer flowers
Penstemon spp.	Beard-tongue	Tall perennial with long-lasting summer flowers
Phlox spp.	Phlox	Flowers most of the growing season; multitude of colors, habits
Rosmarinus officinalis	Rosemary	Tender ev. herb with blue flowers
Salvia spp.	Sage	Low-growing herb
Weigela spp.	Weigela	Large dec. shrub with spring flowers

To provide an attractive environment for hummingbirds, make sure your garden has sources for clean water and a variety of nectar-producing plants. If no natural nectar is available, fill a clean hummingbird feeder with one part sugar to five parts boiled and cooled water and place it in a shady spot. Wash the feeder and change the mixture daily to prevent liver disease in the hummingbirds. If you hang a piece of fruit nearby, the hummingbirds can also eat the fruit flies it attracts. Planting conifers in your garden provides sap for them to drink.

Welcoming Butterflies into Your Garden

Nowadays we seldom see great fluttering clouds of butterflies hovering over the wild landscape. Depleted foraging habitats, along with widespread use of pesticides and herbicides, make natural butterfly-friendly environments increasingly rare. Gardeners can fill an important niche in the butterfly life cycle by providing areas in their gardens for resting, drinking, and feeding.

PLANTS FOR ATTRACTING BUTTERFLIES

SPRING

Arabis spp.	Rockcress	Low, flowering perennial
Aquilegia spp.	Columbine	Spurred and trumpeted blooms
Aubretia spp.		Low, mat-forming perennial
Clematis spp.		Vine with sheltering foliage, flowers
Dianthus spp.	Pinks	Fragrant, starry blooms
Heuchera sanguinea	Coral bells	Low perennial with attractive foliage
Iberis spp.	Candytuft	Low ev. perennial
Lavandula spp.	Lavender	Fragrant, spiky blooms
Primula spp.	Primrose	Shy, woodsy bloom
Tagetes spp.	Marigold	Garden stalwart with bright blooms
Syringa spp.	Lilac	Fragrant dec. shrub

PLANTS FOR ATTRACTING BUTTERFLIES (cont.)

SUMMER

Asclepius tuberosa	Butterfly weed	Tall flowering perennial; strong butterfly attractant biennial; needs wind shelter
Alcea spp.	Hollyhock	Spired biennial; needs wind shelter
Buddleia spp.	Butterfly bush	Rangy dec. shrub, pretty blooms
Clematis spp.		Variety of bloom colors
Echinacea spp.	Purple coneflower	Tough perennial, takes drought
Heliotropum arborescens	Heliotrope	Tender perennial with fragrant blooms
Lilium spp.	Lilies	Bulbs with highly fragrant trumpet blooms; good potted
Lonicera spp.	Honeysuckle	Vine with fragrant blooms, variety of colors
Tagetes	Marigold	Garden stalwart with bright blooms
Nicotiana spp.		Intensely fragrant blooms; grow as annual
Petunia spp.		Colorful, easy annual
Phlox spp.		Variety of bloom colors, habits
Verbena spp.		Perennials and annuals; variety of bloom colors, habits

FALL

Aster spp.		Flowering perennial in variety of bloom colors, habits
Caryopteris spp.	Bluebeard	Small dec. shrub with blue flowers
Echinacea purpurea	Purple coneflower	Tough perennial, takes drought
Tagetes spp.	Marigold	Garden stalwart with bright blooms
Petunia spp.		Colorful, easy annual
Phlox spp.		Flowers most of the growing season; multitude of colors, habits
Sedum spectabile	Stonecrop	Flowering perennial with interesting foliage
Solidago spp.	Goldenrod	Medium perennial with sprays of gold flowers

Butterflies prefer blooms with flat surfaces to perch on while they feed; lavender, pink, white, and yellow are their favorite colors. They require a constant source of nectar from spring through fall, so try to select butterfly-attracting plants according to season of bloom. (For other butterfly-landscaping ideas, see the checklist at the end of this chapter.)

Restoring a Salmon Habitat at Woods Creek Farm

Daryl and Sherrie Parker's Garden
Monroe, Washington

GARDEN SITE	*Partially wooded rural area*
TOPOGRAPHY	*Mostly level bottomland in a river valley; salmon-bearing natural stream winds for half a mile through the property; adjoining the stream are two artificial ponds 10–12 ft. deep for raising fish*
SOIL	*Good, fertile, river-bottom valley soil*
LIGHT	*Sun throughout the day*
AVERAGE ANNUAL RAINFALL	*45 in.*
AVERAGE MINIMUM TEMPERATURE	*45° F (7.2° C)*
MAINTENANCE	*Low*

❧ RESTORING A SALMON HABITAT AT WOODS CREEK FARM

Daryl and Sherrie Parker's Garden
Monroe, Washington

Woods Creek begins as a spring-fed rivulet in the Cascade foothills, widens into a shallow creek as it meanders through the Monroe Valley, and then joins the broad waters of the Skykomish River about 10 miles downstream from its point of origin. Historically, Woods Creek was a rich spawning ground for coho salmon, but over time, as development altered the stream and threatened their habitat, the fish population began a significant decline.

In 1988 Daryl and Sherrie Parker bought a 30-acre farm in the Monroe Valley to serve as a dressage facility for show horses. Because Woods Creek ran for half a mile through their new property, the Parkers decided to rehabilitate the stream and its banks in order to enhance the failing salmon runs.

They began by removing the tangle of blackberry vines that covered the sloping banks of the stream; in their place the Parkers interplanted shrub willows, redtwig and yellowtwig dogwoods, vine maples, and alders in order to create a "tunnel of vegetation" along the stream. Wildlife biologists say these tunnels serve several functions, including stabilizing banks to minimize streamside erosion; creating a shady canopy over the stream to keep the water cool for fish; and supporting an insect population to feed the fish.

When windstorms toppled some nearby alders into the stream, the Parkers left the trunks where they fell in order to provide fish and insects with cover at, and just under, the surface of the water.

Next Daryl improved the streambed for fish habitat by installing rough dams of woody debris to slow the current down at certain spots, thereby creating small pools to serve as spawning beds. He covered the bottoms of these spawning pools with gravel, which provides a prime habitat in which fish eggs can mature and hatch.

A pair of resident mountain beavers helped the rehabilitation efforts along by creating a few spawning-pool dams of their own, composed of woody debris culled from their streamside tree-felling. Since these trees included many of the valuable birches, pines, and fruit trees originally planted near the stream, Daryl replanted the devastated areas with shrub willows, vine maples, and redtwig and yellowtwig dogwoods, shrubs which in his experience the beavers find unsavory.

The Parkers also created two 12-foot-deep artificial ponds on their property, one for rearing salmon fingerlings and the other for raising cutthroat trout. (There are two on-site sources for water for the ponds: in summer, the Parkers pump water from Woods Creek, and in winter, they collect spring water from nearby hillsides and pipe it to the ponds.)

The upper pond, rimmed with rocks and cattails, is stocked with Kamloops trout. The Parkers enjoy fly-fishing here, and they willingly allow the odd bald eagle or kingfisher who occasionally shows up a share of the harvest. The lower pond holds coho salmon, and every January the Parkers invite local fourth- and fifth-graders to release into the pond the fingerlings they have raised as class projects.

Daryl says he enjoys watching the life cycle of the salmon as it unfolds in the waters of Woods Creek. It starts in mid-October, when the salmon swim upstream to spawn; continues in November and December, when the

eggs hatch; and then carries on into spring, as the young fish migrate downstream to live in the ocean for two or three years. Then the cycle begins all over again, as the mature salmon start journeying upstream in fall, to lay eggs in the very gravel beds from which they hatched.

This salmon odyssey—which is probably the most primal drama played out each year in the Northwest's ecosystem—is disappearing from the landscape at a frightening pace. And despite many experiments in different ways to restock the salmon runs in streams, experts are still far from arriving at a consensus on the best way to do it. The current debate, for example, rages over whether hatchery-bred salmon, introduced into the streams by humans, can adequately replace the wild salmon stocks, or whether efforts should mainly be directed at preserving and rebuilding the wild runs of salmon.

Whatever the eventual outcome of this issue, it is still the commitment and efforts of individuals living on salmon-bearing streams, like Daryl and Sherrie Parker, that will prove crucial to preserving salmon runs throughout the Northwest in the coming years.

Above: Salmon have swum upstream to spawn in Woods Creek every fall in increasing numbers since the Parkers began their habitat rehabilitation efforts in 1988.

Opposite page: The Parkers' trout pond in October, when redtwig dogwoods (Cornus stolonifera) *flame across the water's surface.*

NATIVE TREES AND SHRUBS FOR RESTORING THE BANKS OF SALMON-BEARING STREAMS AND PONDS

Acer circinatum	Vine maple	Shrubby, small tree with good fall color
Alnus rubra	Red alder	Quick-growing, moisture-loving tree
Cornus stolonifera	Redtwig dogwood	Medium-sized dec. shrub with attractive red bark in winter
C. s. 'Flaviramea'	Yellowtwig dogwood	As above, except that twigs are bright lemon yellow
Salix spp.	Willows	Moisture-loving trees and shrubs in variety of sizes

CHECKLIST FOR CREATING A NORTHWEST WILDLIFE-ATTRACTING GARDEN

Wildlife will be attracted to gardens with naturalistic, informal planting schemes that feature several distinct "refuge" areas sited well away from the house and from high-use garden zones. These refuges should feel sheltered and secluded, and provide easy access to fresh water. Because pesticides and herbicides potentially are harmful to a wide variety of animals, birds, and insects, they should seldom if ever be used in a wildlife garden.

If you want to attract a range of wildlife, design your garden to include several different kinds of habitats—for example, a woodland area with trees, shrubs, and groundcovers for birds, bats, and small mammals; an open "meadow" area planted with nectar-bearing plants for birds, bees, and butterflies; a woodland edge for birds and small mammals; a pond/stream/wetlands area for fish, amphibians, and birds; and a sheltering thicket for birds and small mammals. This checklist gives specific suggestions on landscaping to attract birds, butterflies, and amphibians.

Attracting birds into your garden:
- Introduce water into your garden by adding a pond, a stream, or a birdbath. Birds like to drink and bathe in

water no deeper than 3 inches, so if you have a deeper water feature, make it more attractive to thirsty birds by adding stones or gravel on which they can perch while drinking. Site the water feature in an open area so that birds can watch out for predators.

Birds like running water better than still water; if adding a stream or a recirculating fountain to your garden is not feasible, then consider installing a bucket of water with one small hole in its bottom over your water feature—the slow but steady drip will attract birds.

Although Pacific Northwest winter weather rarely stays cold enough to freeze water features over for any length of time, remember that birds still need a steady source of fresh water throughout the winter months.

Birds like to bathe in dust as a way to control parasites in their feathers—or perhaps just because it feels good! Install a dust bath in an open, predator-safe site by digging an area in the ground 6 inches deep, lining it with gravel or stones, and then filling it with equal amounts, mixed together, of sand, ash, and soil.

- The best way to provide natural sources of food for birds in your garden is to plant a carefully balanced selection of trees, shrubs, and groundcovers that provide nuts, fruits, and seeds throughout the year. But if you want to supply birds with "boughten" provisions, bird feeders in a multitude of styles (each designed to attract certain birds and to repel others) are available on the market. Contact your local Audubon Society chapter for information on which types of bird feeders and bird seed are appropriate for the specific bird populations you want to attract.

- "Layer" your garden to provide birds with a range of places to perch and forage. Some bird species may live exclusively in woodlands, feeding by scuffling up groundcovers for seeds and fruits, and then roosting high in the branches of the trees above at night. Other species may gravitate to more open ground, spending their time in meadows or by rocky outcrops. The more microhabitats and varieties of plants you can provide in your garden, the wider will be the variety of birds attracted to it. (As with natural gardening, however, be

Above: Carefully sited logs and stones slow the rush of water racing between two fish-rearing ponds on Daryl and Sherrie Parker's ranch in Washington's Monroe Valley.

Right: Moist, boggy terrain attracts a wide range of amphibians into a garden.

Opposite page: A narrow channel of water edged with willows (Salix), vine maples (Acer circinatum), and yellowtwig dogwoods (Cornus stolonifera 'Flaviramea') flows into the Parkers' salmon pond.

sure to plant these microhabitats with the appropriate plants. If, for instance, a shrub usually found in sunny open meadows in the wild is misplanted to a shady area of the garden, not only will the plant fail to thrive, but the meadow-loving birds that are attracted to it in its natural environment may be afraid to venture into the denser area.)

Tree snags, brush piles, and vines are especially valuable features for attracting birds, since they provide cover and roosting spots for the birds as well as habitats for the insects they eat.

- Most birds nest either in tree cavities (the hollows inside dead trees and snags) or in tree or shrub branches. If you want to add birdhouses to your garden, consult with your local Audubon Society chapter or other naturalist organization on which sizes and shapes will attract desirable birds.

Attracting butterflies into your garden:

- Butterflies are attracted to open, sunny areas that are sheltered from wind, and they like a mix of plants, including shrubs, flowering perennials and annuals, vines, and grasses. A good design for a butterfly garden will include a bank of sheltering shrubs planted on the windiest side of the site, and an open area that features plants with varying heights and with bloom times ranging from spring to fall.

The butterfly life cycle consists of four stages: egg, larva or caterpillar, chrysalis, and adult. Butterflies lay their eggs in "weed" plants, such as milkweeds, vetches, clovers, nettles, hops, and thistles, and the hatching larvae, or caterpillars, eat the leaves of these weeds, along with the leaves of trees such as poplars, ashes, and willows. So if you want to increase the butterfly population in your garden, let a secluded area revert to a patch of weeds and add a small plantation of saplings selected from the trees listed above. Once the larvae or caterpillars metamorphose into butterflies, they will find the nectar-bearing flowering perennials and annuals you have planted nearer the house in ornamental (weedless) beds.

Because butterflies avoid drinking from open stretches of water, fill birdbaths or other shallow containers with sand and then saturate, but do not cover, the sand with water. Place these containers in open, sunny sites, and keep the water fresh.

Attracting amphibians to your garden:

• Amphibians—which in the Northwest include newts, salamanders, toads, and frogs—mate and lay eggs in water, but otherwise live most of their adult lives on land. They like the cool, moist areas adjacent to ponds, streams, and wetlands, where they can find the snails, slugs, and insects they eat; in turn, they are the prey of birds and small mammals who inhabit the same ecosystem. Most amphibians are nocturnal, so their presence is a secretive, even mysterious, element in a wildlife garden.

You can attract amphibians to your garden by adding a water feature, such as a pond or wetland area. Place rocks, brush piles, snags, and fallen timber on the margins of the water feature, to provide shelter. Site most of the shelter features on the north side of the pond or wetland, where it is moist and shady. Use no pesticides, herbicides, or algicides in or near the water feature. With these features, amphibians most likely will migrate naturally to your site; artificial introduction may be necessary in highly urban settings.

3

DESIGNING GARDENS
WITH HARDSCAPES

HARDSCAPES—PATHS, terraces, fences, gates, fountains, arbors, and other garden structures—create the signature images we associate with many of the world's great garden design traditions. When we think of

Italian Renaissance gardens, for instance, it's the splashing fountains, tiered and scalloped as wedding cakes, and the dramatic flights of stone steps swirling up steeply wooded hillsides that always seem to leap to mind first. Formal French gardens, on the other hand, conjure up images of graveled grand *allées* cutting through acres of intricate parterres, looking rather like gray velvet ribbons crisscrossing a green tapestry. In these design traditions, hardscapes boldly dominate and define

their garden spaces, in much the same way that walls and floors delineate the parameters of a house.

In other gardening traditions, hardscapes characteristically serve more subtle functions. In Japanese gardens, for instance, the slow, irregular walking pace imposed by stepping-stone paths makes visitors feel as though they are meandering through the landscape rather than striding over it. And the gates, teahouses, fences, and trellises in Japanese gardens often are made of split bamboo or unplaned wood—materials so barely altered from their natural state that they blend back into the garden, rather than standing out against it in sharp relief.

Perhaps it's because the Pacific Northwest is so strongly influenced by Japanese garden design, or maybe it's just that the region's indigenous architectural style is understated— whatever the reason, in the past our garden hardscapes have tended to make low-key design statements rather than bold ones. That's why, when we think of a traditional Northwest garden, what usually comes to mind are images of conifers, rhododendrons, and other woodsy shrubs arranged in informal planting schemes, with hardscapes playing rather minor supporting roles in the overall design.

Of course, there are plenty of exceptions to this generalization, as some of the gardens in the chapters that follow demonstrate. The Mediterranean- and tropical- inspired hardscapes in the gardens of Thomas Hobbs and Brent Beattie (Chapter Five) and David Lewis and George Little (Chapter Six) prove, for instance, that regional design has been taking a dramatic swing in recent years.

Whatever their styles, hardscapes must serve a variety of practical and aesthetic roles in order to function as successful design elements in the garden. This chapter presents three gardens that demonstrate how hardscapes can be used to solve some common landscaping problems.

❧ VIGNETTES, VISTAS, AND VEILS
Stephanie and Larry Feeney's Garden
Bellingham, Washington

The Feeney garden was created in response to a disaster— a disaster that at first brush made Stephanie and Larry feel that they had lost any prospects of having a real garden at all. Hardscapes played a crucial role in creating the new Feeney garden—they became the "architectural elements," in Stephanie's words, around which the rest of the new garden was eventually to coalesce.

The disaster was one faced by many Northwest homeowners: a previously secluded garden, surrounded by either natural forest or mature plantings, suddenly becomes painfully, nakedly, exposed because of the wholesale development of adjoining properties. Everything that made the old garden precious—its privacy, its visual restfulness, and its atmosphere of peaceful enclosure—is destroyed, and the grieving gardener wonders whether the newly transformed space can ever feel like an integrated landscape again.

When the Feeneys bought their property on Lake Whatcom in the mid-1980s, it featured a story-book craftsman's cottage with grounds that were planted in a traditional Northwest mix of mature conifers, rhododendrons, and lawns, all of them set in a large stand of mature second-growth forest. At the time of purchase, Stephanie, a garden writer whose background includes both landscape architecture and graphic arts, felt the garden possessed a "visual and emotional unity," created mostly by the tall trees and hedges enclosing the property and by a rolling lawn that linked the house to the surrounding vegetation.

Within several years, however, the forest that lay outside their front door was bulldozed and a community of a dozen new homes was built in its place. Now the Feeneys had lost the atmosphere of seclusion and the visual tranquility that characterized their old garden, and they faced the challenge of

Vignettes, Vistas, and Veils
Stephanie and Larry Feeney's Garden
Bellingham, Washington

GARDEN SITE	*A 1-acre country garden on the banks of Lake Whatcom*
TOPOGRAPHY	*A level U-shaped front garden 30 ft. deep by 90 ft. wide, which begins to slope down around the the house as it approaches the lake*
SOIL	*Heavy clay, deeply amended*
LIGHT	*Variable throughout the day, with many garden areas receiving sun for no more than several hours*
AVERAGE ANNUAL RAINFALL	*32 in.*
AVERAGE MINIMUM TEMPERATURE	*37° F (2.8° C), with occasional arctic winds raking across Lake Whatcom in winter*
MAINTENANCE	*High throughout the growing season*

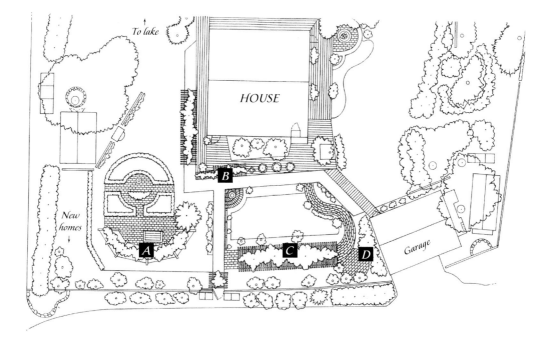

Above: Stephanie and Larry Feeney's garden

creating another one with a new, and necessarily different, personality.

The first new garden structure was a trellis (see point A on the Feeney garden plan, above), which the Feeneys sited in the middle of the front garden lawn to achieve several purposes. On a practical level, they wanted an open, sunny spot for growing kiwi vines, and a trellis seemed the logical structure on which to train them. Also, from a design point of view, the Feeneys thought that a curved trellis would be a good backdrop against which they could plant a new herb garden, especially if a garden bench were placed in front of it with a view looking back across the length of the garden toward the lake. Finally, Stephanie says, "The curving trellis was meant to act as an embrace. I thought of it as having arms that would envelop us and direct our attention (actual and emotional) from the destruction of the forest we had loved and focus it [in the opposite direction] . . . on the peaceful lake."

Using a single structure to address a variety of problems in a garden space, as the Feeneys did with the kiwi trellis, makes that structure so integral to the overall design that it can never look either fussy or absentmindedly tacked on—which are, after all, the two cardinal sins to avoid in adding hardscapes to the landscape.

Once the trellis and the herb garden were successfully installed, the Feeneys began to see more opportunities for transforming their trees-shrubs-and-lawn landscape into a series of garden rooms, with garden structures defining their boundaries. Their next project was a complex of planter boxes and screens (point B on the garden plan) that was meant to close off their front porch from views of the new housing development; at the same time it helped to make the porch area itself feel enclosed so that it could become a new garden space with its own integrity and atmosphere. Small trees planted in Chinese pots and vines scrambling up the screens also helped to create a unique style and mood in the porch area.

VINES FOR COVERING GARDEN STRUCTURES

Actinidia spp.	Kiwi vine	Dec., rampant grower, needs sun and rich soil; "wild, humorous growth, like a dancer"
Ampelopsis brevipedunculata	Blueberry climber	Dec., vigorous, to 15 ft., takes sun or shade; "exquisite foliage and fall porcelain-blue berries"
Clematis alpina	Clematis	Dec., blooms in spring, requires cool roots and sun on blooms
Clematis macropetala 'Bluebird'	Clematis	"Gay little Wedgwood-blue flowers, blooms like a fool in early spring"
Humulus lupulus	Golden hops	Dec., grows to 20 ft. in a season; needs lots of water, sun; "glorious color, a handsome mingler"
Ipomoea spp.	Morning glory	Dec., needs sun; "the annual forms make fabulous screening plants, with heart-shaped flowers in saturated, mouthwatering colors"
Wisteria spp.	Wisteria	Dec., divided leaves and dangling blooms; "elegant and graceful"

A third major project, the grape arbor (point C on the garden plan), also was constructed as a visual barrier to the view along the newly developed side of the property. Stephanie says of the arbor's design: "I realized, as we were making decisions about how tall . . . and long it should be, that by extending its length and following the property [line] we could exaggerate a small curve and thus create a tunnel that would intrigue [visitors] to walk to the end to see what there was to discover." A small brick terrace with seating (point D on the garden plan) serves as a satisfying destination point at the end of the tunneled arbor, although, as Stephanie notes, in actuality the arbor path continues past the terrace room to become a walkway that connects this corner with the rest of the garden.

Above left: An 80-year-old low stone wall leads to the Feeneys' lakeside garden.

Above right: The arbor leads to a small, sunny sitting area that functions as an antechamber to the larger garden beyond it.

Opposite page: Clematis montana *'Rubens' cascading over the Feeneys' cottage deck, with its spectacular lakeside view.*

Thus the grape arbor performs a number of design tasks: it shields and encloses the perimeter of the garden, it leads to a destination point (the sitting area), and it helps to link together all the "rooms" in the front garden in a circular flow. The arbor also serves as a dandy support and backdrop to vines—a role that other hardscapes in the Feeney garden perform as well.

Stephanie says that vines are especially important additions to her garden because she can use them to soften the structures and to integrate them with the planted beds that surround them. Vines also provide leafy green "veils" through which to view other garden vignettes. (The plant list on page 57 includes Stephanie Feeney's favorite vines, with her comments appended.)

Seven years into its renovation, a new personality has been established in the Feeney garden. A series of interlocking hardscapes now organize the landscape into a succession of sophisticated garden rooms, each with a distinct character of its own. Not only do these structures shield the garden from outside views, they also create an atmosphere of warmth and enclosure within the garden itself. Once again there is an emotional and visual unity to the garden.

❀ MAKING A MINKA

Allan Lobb's Garden
Preston, Washington

The forests of the Hida Mountains in Japan's central Honshu province look a lot like those of the western foothills of Washington State's Cascades—heavy stands of conifers mixed in with patches of deciduous trees and shrubs, all of them shading understories of ferns, wildflowers, and mossy nurse logs. But Japan's forests feature one remarkable difference.

From the sixteenth century through the early nineteenth century, peasants and foresters built rustic farmhouses—called *minkas*—on forested hillsides all over Japan. Because of contemporary sumptuary laws, only local materials and simple building techniques could be used in constructing the minkas.

The resulting structures were dark, drafty, and smoky. They were also so charmingly picturesque, with their hand-hewn posts and beams and dramatically pitched roofs, that today the Japanese treasure the few minkas remaining in existence as precious examples of a folk art that carries national historic significance.

The Hida Mountains, which lie outside the ancient capital of Kyoto, retain more minkas than most other regions of Japan, and when Seattle resident Allan Lobb first visited the area in the mid-1970s he quickly became intrigued by them.

Lobb is the retired executive director of a major Seattle hospital, but folk art is his special love. As the author of the book *Indian Baskets of the Northwest Coast and Alaska* (Alaska Northwest Books, 1990), he demonstrates an appreciation of the great beauty to be found in simple forms, natural materials, and ingenious designs. Lobb finds the same quality of beauty in Japanese folk art, especially in minkas and in the folk art objects—such as storage jars, hand tools, and ironware—traditionally associated with them.

After studying minkas on many subsequent trips to Japan, Lobb decided to re-create one here in the New World. He was inspired to do this, in part, because of the similarities he saw between the forests

---

Making a Minka
Allan Lobb's Garden
Preston, Washington

GARDEN SITE	*Rural property with second-growth forest*
TOPOGRAPHY	*The minka and its garden occupy approximately 1 acre of level-to-sloping woodlands, at an elevation of 1000 ft.*
SOIL	*Forest duff, with some planted areas amended with topsoil mixed with a leafy mulch*
LIGHT	*Overall high shade, with some forest canopy trimmed back to provide pools of sun*
AVERAGE ANNUAL RAINFALL	*42 in.*
AVERAGE MINIMUM TEMPERATURE	*37° D (2.8° C)*
MAINTENANCE	*Minimal, but Allan Lobb visits the birds two or three times a week and maintains the minka on a regular basis*

Above: Japanese black pines "planted" in mounds of stone and moss frame Allan Lobb's minka, functioning in the landscape as if they were living sculptures.

Opposite page: Rustic-looking storage jars, buckets, and bamboo brooms complement the unsophisticated materials and design techniques used to create Lobb's minka.

of the Hida Mountains and the forest that covers 40 acres of property he owns in the western foothills of the Cascades, near Preston, Washington. He knew that if he could construct an authentic minka, he already had the appropriate landscape in which to site it.

With the help of his friend and traveling companion Gene Zema, a Seattle-based architect, Lobb began sketching informal construction plans for a minka. He also started a ten-year process of gathering posts, beams, and flooring from salvage yards in Kyoto. Many of these construction

pieces came from dismantled minkas, with some of the big beams dating from the early nineteenth century.

In 1985, Lobb began to construct the minka. He usually worked on weekends by himself and learned by experimentation. The work was done with hand tools and blocks and pulleys; friends occasionally helped with the heavy moving. Today, with its roof shingles weighted down by stones, and moss and lichens etching the plaster and straw walls, the minka nestles into its forest setting as if it has been there for centuries.

Once the minka was built, the next step was to site hardscapes and garden decorations around it that were especially selected to enhance the minka's character and atmosphere. "I wanted simple, natural materials and styles," Lobb explains, "because anything polished or sophisticated would seem out of place."

Lobb began by gathering boulders found on the property, augmenting them with stones purchased from a nearby stone yard, and piling them together with earth to serve as the planting foundations for mature Japanese black pines, some of which he salvaged from construction sites. These specially selected pines, which he trims and manicures, act as "big bonsai," in Allan's words, and give the minka compound some living sculptures to complement its manmade structures. They also underscore the landscape similarities between the forests of Honshu and those of western Washington.

Many decorative and functional objects associated with historic minkas are scattered around the compound, including stone grinding wheels, granite pavers, and wooden agricultural tools. Six eye-catching storage jars sited around the minka's foundation demonstrate the depth of Lobb's commitment to creating an authentic ambience. The large, rough storage jars, some of which date from the seventeenth century, represent Japan's most famous schools of rustic-style stoneware and ceramics. Each school had a distinctive approach or style in shaping the jars; each also featured a unique variation on the natural ash glaze, much prized by connoisseurs, that is created when heat melts the dust on the inside of the kilns onto the jars being fired.

Lobb also purchased in Japan several old stone lanterns whose wild, primitive charm blends in with the rest of his compound. But when he went to acquire more, he could find only new stone lanterns with the kind of polished, sophisticated look that he consciously avoids. So Allan decided to "construct" additional, more natural-looking, lanterns by stacking mossy stones on top of one another. He then placed them in spots around the compound that Japanese gardeners would traditionally choose, such as entryways, exits, and bends in paths. They are also sited near features, such as moss-covered stumps, that illustrate the natural beauty of the Northwest landscape.

A dedicated amateur ornithologist, Lobb designed and constructed some spacious aviaries behind the minka to house his collections of pigeons, doves, and pheasants. A nearby lean-to is stacked with antique, handmade Japanese bird cages, whose forms and lines he finds as intriguing as those of consciously wrought sculptures.

Today, with the minka, the aviaries, and the surrounding garden-compound as fully realized as an intricate work of art, Allan spends much of his time simply enjoying the atmosphere, visiting the birds, and tidying up. He worries a bit about the decay that inevitably invades untreated wood like that used in the minka, but notes quite cheerfully that "we're all going to rot sometime." Meanwhile, there is next spring to look forward to, when sweeps of *Iris pseudacorus* will fill a water meadow lying near the minka with their delicate, pale yellow blooms.

The exotic charm of a Japanese rural landscape has been re-created in this stretch of western Washington woods, mainly through the use of hardscapes and decorations that unite the minka compound to its natural setting. Lobb's achievement here, in terms of garden design, is to use hardscapes to underscore and enhance latent possibilities in the landscape—to take a familiar setting and call forth new potential in it that still honors its original spirit.

Above: A rough water basin and a lantern (which Allan Lobb assembled, in part, from stones found near his minka compound) look so natural that they almost disappear into the Northwest forest scene. Below: Japanese black pines (Pinus thunbergii) *and Japanese maples planted by Lobb around his minka add an exotic touch to some western Washington woodlands.*

❧ HANDMADE HARDSCAPES

Pamela Georges's Garden
Portland, Oregon

From a bird's-eye perspective, Pamela Georges's garden looks like a meticulously pieced patchwork quilt made of brightly colored and richly textured flowerbeds stitched together by flagstone paths. Like the best kind of home quilter, Pamela is a self-taught craftswoman whose good eye, skillful hands, and careful attention to detail have created a unique and highly personal work of art. And as any artist will attest, choosing the materials with which to express your vision is at the core of the creative process.

Copper arches, covered in roses, provide an airy, informal entry into Pamela Georges's garden.

Pamela began her garden in 1989, when she saw a shaft of sunlight falling in a stand of trees near her newly built house in the hills overlooking Portland and the Willamette Valley. At that time Pamela was already a flower lover, so she cleared some of the trees, and then planted a large cutting border in the sunny glade in order to supply the house with bouquets throughout the growing season.

Within a year, Georges came to believe that the border wasn't a "true" garden, that some element essential to a successfully designed landscape was missing. Because of her background in building construction and interior design, it was natural for Pamela to reach the conclusion that only by adding garden structures, or hardscapes, could she transform the planted bed into a real garden.

Self-motivated and highly energetic, Pamela decided to design and install the hardscapes herself, using commonly available construction materials and basic tools and equipment. Her first step was to design a path system "because the garden needed to be pulled together, it needed some boundaries." Pam envisioned a series of interconnecting flagstone paths that would flow around raised flowerbeds, and she selected a regional basalt, called Camas Gray, from which to build them.

Pamela originally had considered using brick, but decided the resulting paths would look too formal; she wanted a garden whose atmosphere would be "semiformal, but not imposing. I wanted the garden to look like it had been there a long time, like it was weathered and aged."

Camas Gray stone, besides looking less formal and more weathered than brick, comes in sturdy, 2-to-3-inch-thick pieces, which can be laid directly into the ground, without beds of sand and/or mortar to support them. Pamela built the paths herself, hauling in 11 tons of stone by wheel-barrow and digging each piece of stone into the ground individually. Of this phase of the garden's construction, Pamela says, "When I said I wanted

Handmade Hardscapes

Pamela Georges's Garden
Portland, Oregon

GARDEN SITE	*Semirural forested estate*
TOPOGRAPHY	*A level 5000-sq-ft. "circle" set into a forested hillside, with mountain views*
SOIL	*Heavy clay, deeply amended with bark-and-mushroom compost and sand*
LIGHT	*Full sun for most of the day*
AVERAGE ANNUAL RAINFALL	*38 in.*
AVERAGE MINIMUM TEMPERATURE	*36° F (2.2° C) with spring 1½ to 2 weeks later than Portland's because of the higher altitude (900 ft.)*
MAINTENANCE	*High in early spring; approximately 8 hours a week of deadheading and tidying for the rest of the growing season*

stones for my birthday, my husband knew I didn't mean diamonds."

Next, raised beds bordered with stacked stone were installed between the paths, and perennials and annuals were planted in them in richly amended soil. Now that the heart of the garden had been established, Georges turned her attention to the garden perimeters, which still lacked definition. She circled parts of the garden with an informal arrangement of shrubs and wood fences, but decided to mark the points of entry and exit with more eye-catching structures.

First, Pamela constructed an arbor made from pressure-treated fir 4×4s to serve as a central focal point in the new garden space. The arbor, which was stained a light gray to look weathered and to blend visually with the gray path stones, actually leads to Pamela's compost pile, although from inside the garden it looks like an elegant exit.

The garden's entry is a series of copper arches bent over a shallow, semicircular flight of stone steps. Pamela had first planned to construct another wood arbor here, similar in appearance to the exit arbor. But on reflection, she decided that an arbor would look "too rigid and formal for a garden entrance. But I'd always liked the idea of the entry being like a pergola that you could walk under. And copper arches are so lightweight that they almost seem to disappear in the summer, especially when the climbing roses I planted on either side of them almost meet overhead." Pamela finds copper an attractive material to use for trellises, arches, and plant supports because it quickly weathers to a verdigris that complements the plants, wood, and stone in the rest of the garden.

Before she decided to install copper arches at the entrance to the garden instead of a wood arbor, Pamela had designed a curved fir plaque that was to sit on top of the arbor. She had decorated the plaque with flowers and curling leaves which she carved with a drummel, a hand tool rather like a large dentist's drill that is available at woodworking shops. After deciding to install the copper arches

Above: Pamela Georges's garden is partially enclosed by wooden arbors and stone paths.

Below: Pamela designed and built this cedar-and-fir garden bench, and then stained it a pale gray to complement the nearby arbors and stone paths.

Opposite page: Pamela used Camas Gray stone for her garden's paths and terraces and for the rim of the pond.

instead, Pamela took the already carved plaque and "retro-fitted" it to the wood arbor at the exit. Later, she used the same carving technique to decorate the backrest of a wood bench that she constructed to stand near the wood arbor.

Pamela's latest major garden project is a terraced rock-ery, with stairs, that climbs the hill behind her garden. The Camas Gray stone used in the rockery also rims a free-form pool at the base of the hill. Using the same stone for both features ensures a uniformity of color, texture, and shape that creates a sense of visual "flow" in this intensely hard-scaped corner of the garden. If several different hardscape materials had been used here—say, land-scape timbers for the terraces, poured concrete for the pool, and brick for the nearby path—the result would have looked over-busy, even jumbled.

After creating the garden's integral hardscapes from a deliberately limited palette of materials—native gray stone for paths and steps; gray-stained pressure-treated wood for trellises, benches, and fences; and copper piping for arches and fixtures—Pamela was free to add decorations in a variety of complementary materials. Clay pots, sculptures, and a birdbath made from a smooth, stonelike product, and wrought-iron garden chairs add visual richness to the scene, without obscuring the major hardscapes' fundamental unity of material and style. This firm control over the basic design elements works so well that visitors to Pamela's garden feel pleasantly energized—rather than overwhelmed—as they stroll along the paths, all their synapses sparking away at the sensory smorgasbord of stone and water, flower and fragrance, that surrounds them.

CHECKLIST FOR HARDSCAPES

For adding hardscapes to brand-new gardens, keep the following suggestions in mind:

- Perhaps the most fundamental decision to make is whether you want the hardscapes to overtly define the garden spaces or to play a supporting role to natural features already there. Most gardeners elect to use a combination of the two approaches, as conditions in each area of the garden warrant.

- Establish a theme or a mood for your garden, and then match the style and materials of your hardscapes to that dominant theme. For instance, an informal Japanese garden calls for natural stepping stones, bamboo fences, and wooden benches, while a cottage garden calls for crazy paving and curving trellises.

- Don't let subsidiary themes or moods, expressed through hardscapes, distract from or conflict with the dominant established theme. Wrought-iron chairs or a gingerbread gazebo, for example, would detract from the theme of a Japanese garden, while abstract sculptures or low stone lanterns would look out of place in a cottage garden.

For adding hardscapes to already established gardens:

- Match the style and materials of the additions to those of the hardscapes already in place. New additions need not simply copy the older hardscapes, however—they can introduce variations on the dominant theme. For example, if you already have a formal flagstone path near the house and you want to extend that path to an area of the garden that is less formal in tone, then you can "break up" the formal flagstone path as it reaches the naturalistic area by interspersing gravel (always a less formal material than cut flagstone) in random patterns. If you gradually alter the ratio of stone to gravel, so that eventually there are more gravel patches than flagstones, it will subtly underscore the change of mood in the garden from formal to natural without doing violence to the overall visual harmony.

- Maintain the dominant scale or proportion that has already been established. For instance, adding a pond of Olympic proportions to a small garden already planted with dwarf conifers and alpine plants in miniature rockeries would badly upset the garden's established scale.

For adding hardscapes to both new and already established gardens:

- Make sure there is a logical and satisfying purpose for the hardscapes in your garden. For example, paths should either lead somewhere, such as to a viewing spot for a pond, and/or eventually link up with other paths in the garden.

- Design and construct hardscapes in spatial sequences that give the garden visitor a variety of experiences. For example, design a long pergola that feels like an enclosed and shady tunnel so that it flows into an open, sunny terrace with wide views. In this way, you can present visitors with successive experiences of shade and sun, enclosure and openness, and mystery followed by discovery.

- Limit the variety of construction materials used and make sure they complement one another; otherwise, your garden may look too jumbled.

4

WATERWISE GARDENS

THE PACIFIC NORTHWEST is renowned—perhaps the word is notorious?—for its rainy weather. And it's true that our region sprouts slugs, clouds, and umbrellas for eight months of the year. But during the annual dry spell that

runs between June and September, we record far fewer inches of rain than many areas on the East Coast and in the Midwest.

Traditionally, Northwesterners more or less ignored these annual summer droughts when they planted the rhododendrons and other moisture-loving plants that so characterize our regional gardens. Instead, we coped by trundling out hoses and sprinklers, or by installing automatic irrigation systems.

By the mid-1980s, however, rapid population growth and continued development were beginning to put noticeable strains on regional water sources. Because almost half of the water in home use during the dry period is devoted to watering lawns and thirsty plants, an interest in waterwise gardening—which stresses using plants and gardening techniques that require minimum watering—began to grow. Today there is plenty of information available on waterwise gardening in the

Northwest, but misconceptions about the subject still keep some gardeners from adopting this approach.

The first major hurdle is an aesthetic one. For many Northwesterners, "waterwise gardening" conjures up images of blowing sand, withered succulents, and basking lizards. In reality, waterwise gardens come in many styles—you can adapt waterwise principles to cottage gardens, Japanese gardens, perennial borders, herb gardens, and many other types.

The second concern is horticultural. A palette of waterwise plants would seem to severely restrict the variety

Patricia Campbell's garden on Bainbridge Island, Washington, offers a sweeping view of Puget Sound and is underplanted with colorful, drought-tolerant herbs and perennials.

of trees, shrubs, groundcovers, and flowering perennials that can be added to your landscape. But the Northwest is fortunate in this respect; we can use plants from other parts of the world that experience the same yearly weather patterns that we do—that is, dry summers followed by mild, wet winters. Plants native to the Mediterranean basin and to regions of Chile, Australia, South Africa, and New Zealand, in particular, settle into our climate quite comfortably.

A third concern is that waterwise gardening may be an arcane art, requiring techniques and approaches substantially different from "regular" gardening. In fact, the single most important factor in successful waterwise gardening, besides plant selection, is careful soil preparation—which is, after all, the basis for all good gardening of any kind.

❧ A FRAGRANT AND COLORFUL BEACHSCAPE
Patricia Campbell's Garden
Bainbridge Island, Washington

Patricia Campbell purchased her Bainbridge Island home high on a bluff overlooking Puget Sound for the view rather than because she had any particular plans for gardening. But when she began to create a garden several years after moving in, it was the home, the view, and the island environment that shaped her landscaping vision.

When Patricia acquired the old farmhouse in 1992 it was, in her words, "a dump with a view." Originally built in 1875, the house served as a community post office from 1906 to 1913, and later became a grocery store. By 1992, the house was essentially a ruin, with holes in the roof, windows that were shimmed into place, and an inadequate furnace. Patricia took a year's absence from work and, with the help of an old friend who is a contractor, renovated the house from foundation to roof, doing much of the work herself. The result is a fully restored island farmhouse, with all its cozy charm preserved.

Once the house was finished, Patricia turned to the garden, which consisted at the time of a stunted old apple tree and a single rosebush. At this point, Patricia knew only two things about the new garden she was going to create: there would be no lawn, because she didn't want to "waste time mowing it," and the plants had to be drought tolerant, because her water supply, as is the case in many island communities in the Pacific Northwest, is severely limited.

The front garden sprang from a visit to the Northwest Flower and Garden Show, which is held every February in Seattle. The show's theme that year was waterwise gardening, and Patricia was particularly intrigued by a demonstration garden that featured an old farmhouse on a shingle beach, with swaths of grasses and other waterwise plants running between the house and the water. It had so many points in common with her house and property that she decided to use it as an inspiration in developing her new front garden.

Patricia established the beach ambience in her front garden by advertising in the local paper for "a dead boat for a garden art project." An 80-year-old island resident phoned her

A Fragrant and Colorful Beachscape

Patricia Campbell's Garden
Bainbridge Island, Washington

GARDEN SITE	*A bluff looking over Puget Sound on Bainbridge Island's northeast side*
TOPOGRAPHY	*A level front garden approximately 30 ft. wide by 15 ft. deep, with southern exposure, and a level back garden 50 ft. wide by 30 ft. deep, with northern exposure*
SOIL	*In the front garden, unamended glacial till; in the back garden, the original glacial till was sifted to remove thumb-sized and larger stones, rototilled four times, and deeply amended with topsoil, Steerco mulch, and lime*
LIGHT	*The front garden receives sun throughout the day; the back garden receives morning and early afternoon sun*
AVERAGE ANNUAL RAINFALL	*40 in.*
AVERAGE MINIMUM TEMPERATURE	*40° F (4.4° C), with occasional arctic blasts from the north in winter, and a spring that arrives approximately 2 weeks earlier than the rest of the area because of the garden's proximity to Puget Sound*
MAINTENANCE	*Two or three good weekends of cleanup in spring, and several hours a week of tidying during the rest of the growing season*

Above: Swaths of grays, yellows, pinks, and violets wash over Patricia Campbell's garden floor, on Bainbridge Island, Washington.

Right: Patricia's garden features waterwise plantings and hardscapes, including an old fishing boat slowly sinking into a whirlpool of beach stones.

Opposite page: Waterwise grasses, daylilies, herbs, and heathers nestle into waves of beach stones in Patricia's front garden.

A SAMPLER OF FRAGRANT/FUZZY/FUN
WATERWISE PLANTS FOR A NORTHWEST BEACH GARDEN

Alchemilla mollis	Lady's mantle	1-ft. perennial with highly textured leaves and chartreuse flowers
Euphorbia characias wulfenii	Spurge	3–4 ft. perennial with dusty blue-green leaves
Perovskia atriplicifolia	Russian sage	3–5 ft. perennial with aromatic silver leaves
Phlomis fruticosa	Jerusalem sage	Tall spiky perennial; white, yellow blooms
Salvia leucantha	Mexican bush sage	Arching 3½-ft. perennial with showy flower spikes
Stachys byzantina [*Stachys lanata*]	Lamb's-ears	Woolly gray opposite leaves on 1-ft. stalks

almost immediately to say "I think your boat is in my backyard." Patricia beached the boat near her front porch and covered the rest of the garden space with specimen rocks and cobbles. She is fascinated by rocks and stones, and has accumulated a large collection gathered from beaches and creeks near Hood Canal, Mount Rainier, and the Hoh rain forest. "Rocks, fossils, feathers, seed pods, shells—to me, that is art," Patricia explains.

Next, she planted a shore pine, grasses, and waterwise flowering perennials in the front yard, amending each digging hole with bonemeal and carefully watering the newly established plants with a mister system through their first growing season. Two years on, these plants are watered only if they start showing signs of stress, which happens rarely. Patricia says she knew that she had succeeded in conveying her artistic vision in the front yard when an eight-year-old neighbor said to her one day, "I get it—we're at the beach, and" (pointing beyond the shingle area to the nearby road) "there's the imaginary ocean."

When Patricia turned her attention to the backyard, she asked garden designer Terri Stanley to help her create a waterwise, low-maintenance garden with "year-round green, lots of textures, lots of herbs, and plants that were fragrant. I didn't want to fill the garden with rhodies and azaleas. I wanted plants that are unique and fun—plants that are fuzzy, like lamb's-ears, and plants that rattle in the winter wind, like Jerusalem sage," Patricia says.

Campbell and Stanley created a color palette featuring a variety of greens and purples, ranging from chartreuse and dusty sage to burgundies and plums. They envisioned waves of these colors flowing through the garden in broad horizontal swaths, complementing the waves of water covering the horizon in the background.

Among Patricia's favorite plants in this part of the garden are Mexican bush sage, a 3-foot-tall herb with late-blooming flowers in long purple spikes that looks good planted next to rockroses; lady's mantle, with its pleated, round blue-gray leaves, which self-seeds ferociously throughout the garden; Russian sage, with long silvery leaves that look good through the winter; and *Euphorbia characias wulfenii,* with its brash, brushy leaves and its startling chartreuse blooms.

For fragrance, Cambell and Stanley planted three varieties of lavender, various santolinas, curry plant, and eight varieties of Mexican sage. A soaker-hose system irrigates the back garden when it's needed, but for the most part the garden functions splendidly on the occasional fall of rain.

Because of the back garden's panoramic view of Puget Sound, Patricia positioned artwork in it to enhance the view rather than to compete with it. A pair of metalwork herons by Port Townsend sculptor Shane Miller is profiled against the horizon, while an amethyst-colored viewing globe reflects both the clouds in the sky above and the waters of the Sound below.

The water-and-island ambience that saturates Patricia Campbell's garden derives from the way in which the garden's design components—plants, stone, and artwork—complement their natural surroundings. Both aesthetically and environmentally, the garden fits into the larger landscape. To a Northwest gardener, what can feel more satisfying than that?

❧ WATERWISING A FRONT GARDEN AND PARKING STRIP

Gil Schieber's Garden
Seattle, Washington

Gil Schieber's imagination is so firmly rooted in plants that when he bought a house on an urban lot in Seattle's Ballard neighborhood in 1987 it was only a short time before he had transformed the front yard's sterile stretches of turf into a horticulturist's treasure box, overflowing with plants chosen for their striking textures, forms, and colors.

Originally Schieber planned to create a woodsy landscape for the front garden featuring Northwest natives—vine maples, ferns, salal, and other decorative groundcovers—leavened with some compatible non-natives, such as *Rhododendron schlippenbachii*. His aim at that point was to

Waterwising a Front Garden and Parking Strip	
Gil Schieber's Garden Seattle, Washington	
GARDEN SITE	*Urban lot*
TOPOGRAPHY	*Level garden area with a western exposure, 75 ft. wide by 25 ft. deep*
SOIL	*Highly amended glacial till*
LIGHT	*Full sun throughout the day*
AVERAGE ANNUAL RAINFALL	*34 in.*
AVERAGE MINIMUM TEMPERATURE	*39° F (3.9° C)*
MAINTENANCE	*2½ days of general cleanup in spring; approximately ½ hour a week of tidying during the rest of the growing season*

Left: Gil Schieber transformed his Seattle lot's front garden and parking strip into a waterwise landscape featuring shrubs native to the Mediterranean, fruit trees and shrubs, ornamental grasses, and a variety of colorful perennials.

Opposite page: Carved, stippled, and banded stones add rich colors and textures to the edge of a waterwise planting bed in Patricia Campbell's garden.

TWELVE BEST ORNAMENTAL GRASSES
FOR A NORTHWEST WATERWISE GARDEN

Calamagrostis acutiflora 'Stricta'	Feather reed grass	Tall clumps with arching leaves; summer flowers last through winter
Carex glauca	Blue sedge	Medium mounder; likes dry shade
Carex pendula	Drooping sedge	Semievergreen; pretty flower spikes
Cortaderia selloana	Pampas grass	Tall clumper with soft ivory plumes
Elymus magellanicus	Blue Lyme grass	Medium archer with narrow blue leaves
Festuca scoparia 'Pic Carlit'	Fescue	Small mounder
Helictotrichon aparicus nanus		Wants light shade; best in groups
Koeleria glauca	Blue hair grass	Small mounder with blue leaves
Miscanthus floridulus	Giant miscanthus	Tall clumper with fall flowers
Ophiopogon planiscapus	Black mondo grass	Small tufts of black leaves; a good groundcover
Stipa gigantea	Feather grass	Medium tufter with yellow, loosely branched flower clusters in summer
S. tenuissima	Narrow feather grass	Short, narrow leaves become showy brown in late summer

create a more-or-less-evergreen, drought-tolerant environment that would look "presentable" year-round.

But Schieber, who has a fruit and vegetable production degree from a college of horticulture and farming in Pennsylvania as well as 15 years' experience as a nurseryman in the Northwest, found himself developing a growing interest in Mediterranean subshrubs and ornamental grasses. This new interest led him to turn his front space into a test garden instead, to see which of the many varieties of these plants currently under cultivation worldwide would flourish best in the Northwest.

Before tucking in a single plant, Gil thoroughly amended the garden's soil, a thin and compacted glacial till. First he turned the sod over, chopped it up, and covered it with a foot of compost. Next he planted nitrogen-fixing potatoes and rye grass in the newly turned soil for the

SHRUBS AND TREES FOR YEAR-ROUND
STRUCTURE IN A NORTHWEST WATERWISE GARDEN

Baccharis magellanicus		Extremely tough ev. shrub, good for erosion control
Carpenteria californica	Bush anemone	Medium ev. shrub; fragrant white summer flowers
Ceanothus spp.	Wild lilac	Shrubs of varying heights; need very sharp drainage; shiny, sharp leaves
Cistus spp.	Rockrose	Shrubs 2–5 ft. tall; pretty summer flowers
Convolvulus cneorum	Bush morning glory	Med. ev. shrub with white flowers; attractive silvery foliage
Eleagnus spp.		Ev. shrubs; silver leaves
Erica arborea	Tree heath	Tender, tall ev. shrub; white spring flowers
Genista spp.	Broom	Small dec. shrubs; attractive spiny branches
Helianthemum nummularium	Sunrose	Ev. shrublet with cascades of bright yellow, orange, or pink flowers in early summer
Leptospermum spp.	Tea tree	Tall ev. shrubs; pretty spring blooms in white and red; need sharp drainage
Prunus laurocerasus 'Mt. Vernon'	Cherry laurel	Medium ev. shrub; glossy green leaves

winter season. After turning these crops under the next spring, Gil added potash and potassium to the soil by spreading rock phosphate, granite dust, and greensand, in the quantities of 10 pounds each per 100 square feet of garden space. (Gil currently recharges this supersoil by adding several inches of compost and small, partially degraded wood chips once every two or three years.) Next he established two berms flanking the walkway leading up to the front door, one of them for acid-loving plants—many of them West Coast natives—and the other for plants that thrive in a well-drained, alkaline soil.

In the past eight years, Gil has experimented with growing over a hundred different kinds of ornamental grasses and subshrubs in his front garden, pinpointing their exact cultural needs by systematically varying their soil types,

HERBACEOUS FILLERS AND DECORATIVE
GROUNDCOVERS FOR A NORTHWEST WATERWISE GARDEN

Alyssum spp.		Fragrant, self-seeding; good groundcovers
Campanula spp.	Bellflower	Variety of heights, bloom colors, forms; good minglers
Consolida ambigua	Larkspur	Spiky violet blooms in early summer
Crocus spp.	Crocus	Low bulbs; early spring flowers come in many colors
Dianthus spp.	Pinks	Neat, mat-forming groundcovers; many forms, heights, bloom colors
Iberis spp.	Candytuft	Tough ev. groundcovers; good year-round presence
Lilium spp.	Lilies	Tough, early bloomers, especially the Asiatics
Nigella spp.	Love-in-a-mist	2 ft. tall, spring flowers; nice dainty mingler
Papaver spp.	Poppies	Varying heights, bloom colors
Salvia greggii		4-ft. ev. plant; handsome leaves; pink blooms in spring
Silene spp.		Groundcovers with varying heights, forms, colors

Left and opposite page: Waterwise grasses, groundcovers, and perennials in Gil Schieber's garden.

watering schedules, and exposures to sun and wind and then noting how they respond to the changes.

But this focus on matching plants to their habitats doesn't mean that Gil neglects design considerations when planting his garden. Over the years a lively mix of structural plants (mostly evergreen subshrubs), decorative ground-covers, and what Gil calls "herbaceous seasonal fillers" have taken over the front garden and the parking strip. (The seasonal fillers add color and structural interest around the skirts of the shrubs and grasses.) Along with some fruit-bearing bushes and vines, and some plants chosen for their fragrance, they all tumble together in a Darwinian scramble for survival, with the fittest living on until the next growing season.

The present-day garden is full of hardy, waterwise plants that require little or no watering, fertilizing, or maintenance beyond what nature provides. An astounding diversity of plant life from all over the world set within an attractive planting scheme, Gil Schieber's garden shows us just how far a talented horticulturist can push the limits when designing a waterwise Northwest landscape.

❧ SOFT TEXTURES AND DELICATE COLORS IN A WATERWISE LANDSCAPE

Wendy and Ron Klages's Garden
Lake Forest Park, Washington

From a distance, the garden of Wendy and Ron Klages features many of the soft colors and textures that characterize a classic English perennial border: pastel blooms wash over lacy foliage, with the whole composition glimmering like a delicate watercolor viewed through a mist.

But closer in, a visitor realizes that this garden's plants are on a far more robust scale than those typically found in flowerbeds, with trees, large ornamental grasses, and clumps of shrubs forming its major building blocks. The plants are also tough, drought-tolerant bruisers, selected for their ability to withstand a baking southwest exposure with no irrigation during our region's two-and-a-half-month annual summer dry spell.

So how does the garden area retain its fresh delicacy throughout the summer, given these difficult growing conditions? The answer lies in careful plant selection, with emphasis on waterwise trees, shrubs, and perennials that have graceful foliage and subtle colors.

When the Klageses first bought the property in 1991, the garden was a three-tiered rockery overgrown with blackberries, ivy, and bedraggled hybrid tea roses. Although the rockery was poorly designed and installed, the Klageses decided that ripping it out would be too expensive, so instead they removed the existing plants, thoroughly amended its soil, and concentrated on selecting new plants that would soften and lighten it.

Working with Seattle garden designer Dan Borroff, Wendy chose such trees as golden locusts and the purple-leaved varieties of smoke trees for their delicate foliage, and then underplanted them with large, arching clumps of the ornamental grasses *Eragrostis curvula* and *Deschampsia caespitosa,* whose tapering leaves and graceful flower clusters flow in soft eddies down the slope.

The feathery textures and subtle coloring of locusts, smoke trees, and ornamental grasses dominate the vertical lines of the replanted rockery, but a wide array of subshrubs, herbs, and groundcovers add structure and variety to the horizontal understories. The lacy foliage of artemisias, rue, catmints, and Russian sages show well against the denser

Soft Textures and Delicate Colors in a Waterwise Landscape

Wendy and Ron Klages's Garden
Lake Forest Park, Washington

GARDEN SITE	*Suburban lot*
TOPOGRAPHY	*A fairly steep slope approximately 30 ft. wide by 60 ft. deep*
SOIL	*Thoroughly amended glacial till*
LIGHT	*Full sun throughout the day*
AVERAGE ANNUAL RAINFALL	*40 in.*
AVERAGE MINIMUM TEMPERATURE	*39° F (3.9° C)*
MAINTENANCE	*Two or three weekends in spring spent staking, pruning, and dividing; two or three weekends in fall spent mulching; twice-weekly cleanups (mainly weeding and deadheading) during the rest of the growing season*

Above: Sunlight burnishes ornamental grasses that flow down a dry southwest slope in Wendy and Ron Klages's garden in Lake Forest Park, Washington.
Opposite page: Delicate colors and textures dominate the waterwise perennial borders in the Klages's garden.

WATERWISE PLANTS WITH SOFT FOLIAGE
AND DELICATE COLORING FOR A NORTHWEST GARDEN

Achillea 'Hoffnung'	Yarrow	Pale yellow blooms with ferny leaves
Artemisia absinthium 'Lambrook Silver'	Wormwood	Ev. herb with silver leaves, 2–3 ft.
Artemisia stellerana	Beach wormwood	2-ft. woody herb with woolly gray aromatic leaves
Caryopteris clandonensis	Blue mist	Mounding dec. subshrub with blue flowers late in season
Cotinus coggygria 'Purpureus'	Purple smoke tree	Sml. dec. tree with "puff-of-smoke" seed clusters, purple leaves
Cotinus coggygria 'Royal Purple'	Purple smoke tree	Deeper purple leaves; gray smoke puffs
Deschampsia caespitosa		2-ft. ev. arching grass with tall, feathery flowers
Eragrostis curvula		Low perennial grass with narrow leaf blades
Gaura lindheimeri		Tall, spiky perennial with early white flowers
Gypsophila repens 'Rosea'	Creeping baby's-breath	Low, mat-forming groundcover with pink blooms
Nepeta fassenii 'Six Hills Giant'	Catmint	Tall, dec. perennial with dusty green leaves, blue flowers
Perovskia atriplicifolia	Russian sage	3-ft. dec. perennial with silvery leaves, blue flowers
Robinia pseudoacacia	Black locust	Tall, fast-growing, dec. tree with gracefully drooping gold leaflets
Ruta graveolens	Rue	Aromatic herb with soft blue leaves, 2–3 ft.
Sisyrinchium striatum		1½-ft. irislike perennial with blue leaf blades and yellow flowers

leaves of rockroses, *Ceanothus,* hostas, and small junipers, while half a dozen David Austin and old-fashioned climbing roses add seasonal blooms and fragrance.

Wendy Klages says that this planting scheme, besides looking cool, elegant, and flowing, requires little in the way of upkeep: "I wanted a garden where, if I couldn't get out to weed for a bit, it wouldn't be a disaster." Best of all, the garden requires virtually no watering year-round, except for the spot-watering of newly established plants during their first growing season.

Checklist for Waterwise Gardening

- Start with a good design, which includes the following: terracing or contouring slopes to retain rainwater runoff; establishing thirsty plants at the base of a slope, where they receive maximum benefit from runoff; establishing "water zones" in the garden, grouping together plants with similar water requirements; and growing vegetables and cutting flowers in raised beds for optimal watering efficiency.

- Improve the soil. Adding organic matter—compost, chopped leaves, peat moss, and manures—to soils will improve their ability to hold moisture. At the same time, improved soils drain excess water rapidly, thus helping to prevent the root rot that attacks so many drought-tolerant plants during our rainy Northwest winters.

  Amend your soil in autumn by digging it over 18 inches deep, removing stones and roots, spreading 3–4 inches of good compost over the area, and working the compost thoroughly into the soil.

- Use mulch. Covering a planting bed with 2–3 inches of mulch helps grow healthy plants by retaining moisture, keeping roots cool in hot weather and protected in cold weather, and suppressing weeds. You can use compost, shredded bark, chopped leaves, and many other materials for mulch. Leave a ring several inches wide around the woody stems of plants in order to avoid rot and disease.

- Reduce the size of lawns. Replace high-maintenance, thirsty lawns with drought-tolerant groundcovers and ornamental grasses.

- Select waterwise plants. Many gardeners assume that our native plants, having adjusted to the region's annual cycle of rain and drought, must be the best selections for a Northwest waterwise garden. This is not necessarily the case; recent tests show that waterwise exotics, such

Above: Boulders, pines, and ever-green groundcovers create a tough waterwise "buffer garden" between a cottage on Washington's Hood Canal and the beach.

Left: Glass "stones" by well-known Northwest artist Dale Chihuly add slick gleams to a waterwise area in a garden near Gig Harbor, Washington.

Opposite page: The gold and purple leaves of locusts (Robinia pseudoa-cacia 'Frisia') and purple smoke trees (Cotinus coggygria 'Purpureus') provide canopies for lower-growing gray- and blue-foliaged plants.

as rosemary, thyme, sage, and lavender, survive prolonged regional droughts better than many of our natives.

Newly planted waterwise plants need careful watering during their first, and perhaps second, growing season; remember, they aren't drought-tolerant until they are firmly settled into the garden, with well established root systems!

Many non-native waterwise plants need sharp drainage to survive in the Northwest's soggy winter soils; plant them on slopes or in especially well-amended soils.

- Irrigate efficiently. Whether you use hoses, drip systems, or automatic sprinklers, irrigate at low volume to optimize soil penetration and minimize runoff. Water infrequently but deeply to encourage deep root growth. Water in the morning to reduce evaporation and to prevent the spread of fungus on wet foliage.

- Practice good maintenance. Most drought-tolerant plants require minimal fertilizing and pruning. Other than watering newly established plants, the waterwise gardener's main task is weeding, since weeds compete with more garden-worthy plants for available moisture and nutrition.

5

GARDENS IN
SMALL SPACES

W E PACIFIC NORTHWESTERNERS may live in a massively scaled natural landscape, but many of our gardens—particularly those in urban settings and in newly developed suburbs—are surprisingly small.

The main reason for this paradoxical situation is an economic one. Space is always at a premium in cities, and this is especially true in the Northwest: Seattle, for instance, is squeezed between the ungiving geographical barriers of Puget Sound to the west and Lake Washington to the east. And in the future, as the entire region "infills" with greater population densities, the suburban developments surrounding our other major cities and towns will also feature significantly smaller property lots because of escalating land prices.

But there are other, noneconomic, reasons for the increasing appeal of small gardens: they cost less to install and require less time to maintain. And many gardeners find the challenge of designing a whole world within a small space, complete with its own personal style and atmosphere, to be a real spur to their imaginations.

"Green walls" and lattice fences create privacy and tranquility in an outdoor room in Bill Overholt's Seattle garden, which was designed by landscape architect Robert Chittock.

The major problems designers of small gardens face include:

- Providing the kinds of enclosure, consisting of plants and/or hardscapes, that make a garden feel private and secluded but not walled off

- Creating a series of alternating garden experiences—drama and tranquility, openness and seclusion, closeup and distant views—within a small space

- Establishing a good visual flow between a house and its garden, especially where little physical space exists between them to effect the transition

- Choosing hardscapes that are compatible with one another, since in a small garden they all are likely to be viewed together during one continuous sweep of the eye

- Selecting a palette of plants that remains interesting year-round, because many small gardens are visible from the house during all seasons

❋ BRINGING THE INDOORS OUT

Bill Overholt's Garden
Seattle, Washington

Savoring the cool, classical elegance of Bill Overholt's city garden, visitors may be struck by the crucial role that "green architecture" often plays in successfully designed small urban lots.

An ancient wisteria (left) shelters a walkway leading between Overholt's various garden rooms.

Bringing the Indoors Out

Bill Overholt's Garden
Seattle, Washington

GARDEN SITE	*Urban lot*
TOPOGRAPHY	*A level 45- by 100-foot lot, with the house taking up most of the space; the garden wraps around the house in a series of rooms and pathways bordered by plants*
SOIL	*Good sandy loam; certain areas in the garden have been amended over the years*
LIGHT	*Generally shady, with some sunny spots*
AVERAGE ANNUAL RAINFALL	*40 in.*
AVERAGE MINIMUM TEMPERATURE	*38° F (3.3° C)*
MAINTENANCE	*Approximately three days a year for clipping and pruning the evergreen hedges; several hours a week for sweeping the walks and terraces*

The term "green architecture" refers to the practice of using plants as architectural components in much the same way that fences, walls, and trellises are used—both to enclose an entire garden and to define smaller areas within it.

In larger, nonurban gardens, these functions usually are performed by walls, fences, and other vertical hardscapes, often against a background of leafy greenery. But a small city garden typically has a dense jumble of houses, apartment buildings, garages, and/or alleys serving as its backdrop.

And here the urban gardener faces a major problem. If you construct yet more hardscapes to block out this background, you may well end up with a garden that looks "hard" and feels oppressively overbuilt and closed in. So, although your urban garden has heightened needs for enclosure, boundary definitions, and protection from unsightly views and noise, it's especially important to find a workable alternative to installing more hardscapes—an alternative that will make your haven feel enclosed and protected, and yet "soft" and natural at the same time. And this is where using green architecture comes in.

Bill's garden demonstrates just how effectively this alternative can solve some classic city garden landscaping problems. In its bare bones, the lot has some strong negatives: it's a narrow band of property that wraps around a two-story brick mansion on a busy street; it's surrounded by other tall structures; and it receives little direct sun.

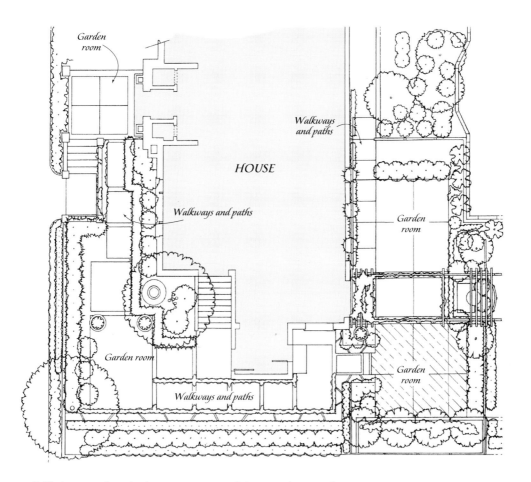

Above: Bill Overholt's garden

Bill has enclosed the perimeter of his garden with banks of clipped evergreen hedges, including hollies *(Ilex),* English boxwood *(Buxus sempervirens),* and Italian cypresses *(Cupressus sempervirens),* which create a vertical green wall that filters out noise and visual pollution from the outside while providing a tranquil and restful backdrop for the spaces it encloses on the inside.

Within the garden, Bill has used airy latticework fences and more evergreen shrubs to shape a series of garden rooms, each of which extends from one of the main "living" rooms of the house—kitchen, study, drawing room—into the outdoors.

These garden rooms, which are sited to make the most of the property's sunny spots, feel spacious and airy, even

Left: Decorative touches show Bill Overholt's attention to detail: the ochre pot and rusted wrought-iron chair are set off by the white chair cushion and marble table top. Green tassels and piping on the cushion repeat the color of the evergreen Japanese holly hedges in the background.

Opposite page: Indoor and outdoor living spaces flow into one another via French doors in Bill's garden.

though their square footage is quite small. This effect has been achieved in several ways.

First, French doors between each garden room and its interior twin make the flow between them easy and inviting: when the French doors are open, the outdoor gardens feel as if they are doubled in size.

Second, smooth textures and cool, receding colors have been used for the hardscapes and plants that furnish each garden room. For example, in the room that landscape architect Robert Chittock designed and installed for Bill (shown on the lower right of the Overholt garden plan), banks of clipped evergreens make a soft, glossy foundation

PLANTS FOR GREEN WALLS

The plants in the following list are evergreen, take pruning reasonably well, and tolerate pollution—qualities that make them prime choices for urban screening. Many also have varieties with variegated leaves—blotched or edged with gold, cream, or silver—that brighten shady garden corners. (Best of all, they're none of them laurel or pyramidalis!)

Aucuba japonica		Fast-growing; tropical-looking leaves; loose habit for informal screening
Buxus sempervirens	English boxwood	Tough 15-foot shrub for dense screening
Choisya ternata	Mexican orange	Needs shelter and rarely grows taller than 7–8 feet, but the foliage is cheerful and starry clusters of fragrant white blooms appear in late spring
Cotoneaster salicifolius	Willowleaf cotoneaster	To 15 ft.; narrow leaves on graceful branches; red berries
Cupressocyparis leylandii	Leyland cypress	Fast-growing to 18 ft.; feathery needles; an alternative to *Thuja pyramidalis*
Eleagnus macrophylla 'Ebbingei'	Silverberry	Silvery foliage; to 10 ft.; red berries
Escallonia spp.		6–15 ft., many varieties; pink/white flowers in late summer; needs sheltered location
Ilex spp.	Holly	Many varieties, 6–15 ft.; attractive berries; dense habit; glossy leaves help brighten a dark area
Juniperus virginiana 'Sky Rocket'	Skyrocket juniper	Junipers come in many sizes and shapes, but this variety is a slim 12-ft. column with striking blue needles
Ligustrum japonicum	Japanese privet	10 ft.; dense foliage; good for topiary
Myrica californica	Pacific wax myrtle	Cheerful, springy foliage; loose screener; grows fast to 6–10 ft., then slowly, reaching 20 ft. in 20 years
Viburnum spp.		Many varieties, 6–15 ft.; most have a loose habit good for informal hedging; nice leaf texture; attractive berries

for the latticework fences that rise above them. The colors of the poured aggregate flooring and the garden furniture echo the gray of the fences; bench cushions, a painted iron table, and ruffled geraniums add fresh white accents. In spring, several magnolias *(Magnolia grandiflora)* and a magnificent

Chinese wisteria *(Wisteria sinensis)* scatter snowy blooms over this garden room, transforming it into a landscape of delicate, fragrant, fleeting beauty.

Walkways connect most of Overholt's major garden rooms, and they serve two valuable functions: the obvious one of providing a continuous circulation flow around the house, and the subtle one of creating experiential contrasts for visitors as they walk between the various garden rooms. Comparatively narrow and lined with plants, the paths make intriguing jogs around building corners, luring visitors to discover the open, sunny garden rooms lying farther on.

Thus the overall garden design exploits the awkward problem of narrow spaces "pinned on" around a tall house by creating walkways and paths in especially narrow areas and using them to connect the garden rooms, which are situated where the garden widens. The paths are used to create a sense of mystery and anticipation, while the garden rooms create several distinct environments and atmospheres within a small space through different light exposures, plant palettes, and sets of decorations.

As a noted Seattle interior designer, Bill Overholt has a discerning eye for the ornamental details that perfect a room, whether it's indoors or out. He has assembled antique garden furniture, statues, and planting pots from several different cultures and centuries that add grace notes to the evergreen walls surrounding the garden. Some, such as a classical bust and a patio fountain, are positioned so that they can be viewed easily from the inside rooms, while others, such as some stone pots, dress up the bare-bones elegance of the evergreen architecture with seasonal color and fragrance.

Bill's use of evergreen plants as architectural components transforms this site thoroughly so that an area that could seem dark, constricted, and closed in instead feels deliciously light, sleek, and spacious. Gardens with such qualities invite their owners to spend as much leisure time as possible outside, blurring the hard distinctions between indoor and outdoor living spaces that so often seem to characterize crowded urban settings.

Parterres and Picket Fences

Sarah Pearl's and Barry Sacks's Garden
Bainbridge Island, Washington

GARDEN SITE	*Rural garden on Bainbridge Island*
TOPOGRAPHY	*A level rectangle 70 ft. long by 30 ft. wide, on the east side of the house*
SOIL	*A good light texture; planting beds are top-dressed with mushroom compost every spring*
LIGHT	*Full sun from morning until midafternoon*
AVERAGE ANNUAL RAINFALL	*40 in.*
AVERAGE MINIMUM TEMPERATURE	*High 30s F (around 3.3° C), but this garden is a bit colder than the land surrounding it because it sits on top of a hill and also lies below the level of the house deck, so cold air tends to get trapped*
MAINTENANCE	*One day in spring for top-dressing the beds; two or three days in fall to clean beds and remove leaves; about four hours a week during the rest of the growing season to deadhead, weed, and clip the boxwoods*

❧ PARTERRES AND PICKET FENCES

Sarah Pearl's and Barry Sacks's Garden
Bainbridge Island, Washington

Parterres—flowerbeds and paths arranged in patterns—had their beginnings in such formal landscaping styles as the chateau gardens of seventeenth-century France, where sculpted rows of evergreen plants set among graveled paths enclosed geometric planting beds of flowers and herbs. Sharp lines and clipped edges, rather than the floppy flow characteristic of natural plant growth, dominated these formal parterres.

Right: A parterre defines the entry room to Sarah Pearl's and Barry Sacks's Bainbridge Island, Washington, garden.

Opposite page: The arbor, designed and built by Barry, sports Rosa 'Dortmund', which Sarah describes as "a perfect rose for the Northwest" because it is a repeat bloomer, requires little fussing, and is highly resistant to black spot and mildew.

In contrast, picket fences fall into a style that can best be described as casual and informal. They seem expressly designed for holding back the scrambling roses and charmingly disheveled clumps of herbs, annuals, and flowering perennials usually associated with cottage gardens.

Mixing two such defining examples of formal and informal garden hardscaping could be a little tricky, especially in a constricted area. Yet in Sarah Pearl's and Barry Sacks's garden it succeeds admirably. So why does this bit of design heresy work? And what lesson does it hold for other gardeners working with small spaces? First of all, let's look at the functions that both elements perform in the design.

The garden acts as the front entry to the house, a cedar-shingled cottage with high, paned windows and a spacious front deck. When Sarah and Barry moved onto the property in 1989, the front garden consisted of several perennial beds overshadowed by a huge madrone. Almost immediately, they began to change the garden to reflect their own tastes and interests.

Barry is a first-rate cook who likes to grow his own herbs, and since the kitchen is located near the entryway, he wanted an herb garden sited just outside the front door. Sarah likes working with the ornamental possibilities of herbs, so it was important to her that this garden area work aesthetically as well as functionally. In fact, since the herb garden would, in effect, be the entry point to their home, both Barry and Sarah felt it was important that the garden have a "hint of formality" and also look interesting year-round.

They chopped the madrone down (its stump still functions as a step to the front deck) to bring more sun in and converted the perennial beds to box-lined parterres filled with herbs, roses, and other blooming plants. These parterres, which form five separate planting beds, perform several functions. First, from a design perspective, they break up the garden rectangle into smaller units of space. And as with interior design, where furniture makes a small room look larger, filling up a garden space with smaller units makes it look larger.

Second, the parterres add some intricate lines and shapes to the simple rectangle; the central parterre, filled with roses and lavenders, creates a strong focal point, while the corner parterres, facing each other on diagonals, set up interesting sight lines and perspectives to the rest of the garden as you tread the gravel paths that border them.

The parterres also serve as a handy way to segregate plants according to their watering needs: drought-tolerant rosemarys, culinary thymes, oreganos, and santolinas fill one bed, while thirstier plants, such as roses and peonies, are planted in another. Finally, the box-lined parterres provide year-round formal structure in the garden, since their patterns remain decorative even in the dormant season.

The picket fences also play a crucial role in this garden's plan. Since the herb garden is only one "room" within a much larger garden, Sarah and Barry constructed a fence around it to firmly demarcate its boundaries; by using a picket fence and open arbors, they underlined the enclosed area's design associations with herb and cottage gardens. Paradoxically, although the picket fence marks off the herb garden from the larger garden space, its slats create a see-through barrier that comfortably integrates the smaller unit into the overall landscape.

For additional formality, structure, and visual richness, Sarah has added pieces of garden art to the enclosed area. Perhaps the most immediately eye-catching are two topiary elephants, which Sarah fashioned from clothesline wire covered in chicken wire and then filled with sphagnum moss. The larger elephant balances on a circus ball covered in vinca, while the smaller one has ivy twining over its frame. Here again, Sarah has used a classically formal element—topiary—in an informal manner to add both structure and whimsy to her garden.

Large planter boxes and pots hold a variety of colorful and fragrant plants throughout the growing season, beginning in spring with crocuses, daffodils, and tulips, and then

moving on to scented geraniums, verbenas, and lobelia in summer. (After the bulbs bloom in the containers, they are planted out in the garden for the next spring. Because Sarah likes to use the same varieties of bulbs each year, the garden is gradually building up sheets of blooms whose colors coordinate with those in the containers—another formalizing touch.)

Sarah and Barry's garden plan successfully mixes formal and informal design elements in a small space. They have directed both the informal and the formal to serve their overall plan—to demarcate boundaries, to create year-round structure, and to add visual intricacy. The dominant herb and rose plantings, which conjure images of both traditional and informal cottage gardens, bridge two otherwise opposing design motifs. Sarah and Barry creatively prove that even garden design rules are meant be broken!

Above: A picket fence, flanked by cottage-garden perennials and annuals, creates a see-through boundary between the entry garden and the larger grounds that surround it.

Opposite page: A topiary elephant constructed by Sarah salutes a stand of herbs and perennials in a corner parterre.

❧ A VILLA IN VANCOUVER

Thomas Hobbs's and Brent Beattie's Garden
Vancouver, British Columbia

Although Pacific Northwest gardeners have been experimenting with individual plants native to the Mediterranean for many years, we've been slower to adopt the Mediterranean garden style as a whole.

In the mind's eye, this look includes smooth, stucco walls painted in warm peachy colors, enclosing paver-flagged terraces that overlook sweeping views of hills and water. Spiky palms in terra-cotta pots are set among beds of santolinas, euphorbias, verbascums, and roses; water lilies crowd pools tiled with cool celadon mosaics. Pungent woolly thymes creep between the terrace pavers, while Oriental lily trumpets, half-stupefied by their own heavy fragrance, droop over beds of blue- and silver-foliaged plants.

A little too exotic for our low-key Northwest tastes? Thomas Hobbs and Brent Beattie don't think so, and as designers of imagination and plantsmen of skill, they have created just such a garden perched on a cliff in a Vancouver, British Columbia, neighborhood overlooking English Bay and the Coast Mountains.

The garden perfectly complements the villa-style home it surrounds. Thomas Hobbs and Brent Beattie, the owners of Southland Nursery in Van-

---

A Villa in Vancouver

Thomas Hobbs's and Brent Beattie's Garden
Vancouver, British Columbia

GARDEN SITE	*An urban lot with views of mountains and English Bay*
TOPOGRAPHY	*Steeply sloping triangular lot, with the front property line 350 ft. long and two side property lines 300 ft. long*
SOIL	*A naturally good, fairly acidic garden soil, equal parts clay, sand, and loam; occasionally top-dressed with manure*
LIGHT	*The front garden has an open western exposure and receives full sun throughout the day; the terrace has a southeast exposure and receives late morning to evening sun*
AVERAGE ANNUAL RAINFALL	*58.7 in.*
AVERAGE MINIMUM TEMPERATURE	*36° F (2.2° C)*
MAINTENANCE	*Continual maintenance throughout the growing season*

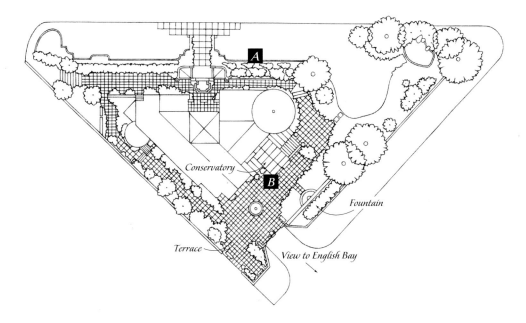

Above: Thomas Hobbs's and Brent Beattie's garden

couver, acquired the house in 1990 because they loved its Mediterranean look, but it took a thorough renovation of the old structure, which had been built in the late 1920s by contractors imported from the film studios of Hollywood, to bring out its exotic possibilities.

Because the building dominates its lot, finding the right colors for its walls and trim was crucial; Thomas and Brent tried 13 different combinations before selecting a soft peachy pink (Thomas, a dyed-in-the-wool Northwesterner, calls it "salmon") for the walls and a celadon blue-green for the trim. "These Mediterranean colors look very subtle and soft in Northwest rain, they don't glare at all," Thomas notes.

Once the house was painted, Thomas and Brent concentrated on bringing out the exotic aspects of the landscape. The existing garden featured traditional Northwest favorites such as rhododendrons, ferns, and other woodland plants. But sprinkled among them were some plants, many of impressive size and maturity, that could lend themselves to a Mediterranean look. These included a stand of towering Lawson cypress *(Chamaecyparis lawsoniana),* a 60-year-old fig tree, and a hedge of golden cypress.

Above: The largest "room" in Thomas's and Brent's garden is the front entry, where sweeping lawns and a deep border create a grand effect.

Using these plants as a structural backdrop, Thomas and Brent tore out the rhododendrons and other shrubs that had strong Northwest associations, replacing them with evergreens, such as fatsias, mahonias, and hellebores, that are able to assume a Mediterranean look when given a sympathetic context.

Today, the major garden areas with Mediterranean-style hardscapes and plants are a roomy border, 10 feet wide by 40 feet long, in front of the house, which faces west (see point A on the garden plan), and a terrace in the back garden complete with views, a lion's-head fountain, and a conservatory (see point B on the garden plan).

The scale and tone of the front border are set by large foliage plants with Mediterranean associations, among

them windmill palms, honeybush *(Melianthus major),* and yuccas, but some small architectural gems such as hebes and echeverias also reside here. Most of these plants have blue, gray, silver, and mauve undertones, which play off the house's salmon stucco walls beautifully. Blooming plants include poppies, euphorbias, daylilies, and yarrows, whose flowers range the color spectrum between peaches, oranges, and pale golds. These dramatic color combinations look rich rather than hectic because Thomas follows a self-imposed rule of using no more than three colors in a specific planting arrangement and "avoiding color combinations that look like pizza."

The terrace, which was built on 11-foot-high retaining walls, continues the Mediterranean theme with planting

Tiles, mosaics, warm stucco walls, and plants with gray and blue foliage create a Mediterranean atmosphere in Thomas Hobbs's and Brent Beattie's Vancouver garden.

PLANTS FOR A MEDITERRANEAN-STYLE GARDEN

Allium spp.		Globular blooms in lilac, blue, rose, or white on stalks from 9 in. to 3 ft.; poor soil and little water produces lots of blooms
Artemisia spp.		Foliage plants with silvery gray leaves; aromatic; 2–4 ft.
Ballota pseudodictamnus		2-ft. mounder with compact, silver-green leaves
Euphorbia myrsinites		Sprawling 1-ft. groundcover with stubby gray-green leaves and chartreuse spring blooms
Hebe cupressoides		Rounded ev. shrub 2–3 ft. tall, with dense, springy leaves
Melianthus major		5-ft. shrub with gray-green, fringed foliage; great presence in a mixed border; fairly tender
Santolina chamaecyparissus		2-ft. mounder with aromatic silver needles; needs hard pruning in early March; *S. virens* has light green leaves that are softer and more ferny
*Sedums spp.		Low-growing succulents with fascinatingly architectural structures; use as groundcovers and fillers
Thymus pseudolanuginosus	Woolly thyme	Neat, thick, tiny gray leaves, 1–3 in. high; good for pavement cracks
Trachycarpus fortunei	Windmill palm	Shaggy, hairy trunk with a mop top of shiny, pleated leaves; protect trunk in cold weather, plant out of wind, and this palm does well in maritime Northwest
Yucca spp.		Spiky evergreen shrubs 2½–10 ft. tall; use for year-round structure

*See also the plant lists in Chapter Four for other plants suitable for a Mediterranean-style garden.

beds filled with roses, lilies, ornamental grasses, iris, peonies, and sempervivums. Formal touches are introduced by the water-lily pool and by some handsome urns and terra-cotta pots filled with ornamental grasses such as *Stipa tenuissima;* trailing groundcovers and vines crawl over the rims of the pots with an almost theatrical vigor.

In fact, the whole terrace is theater, from the dramatically simple backdrop of walls, water, and sky to the carefully selected foreground "props" of urns and architectural plants. Small spaces, whether they be stages or gardens, force us to focus on a relatively few design elements, which we must then use to maximum effect. The dominant impressions in Thomas's and Brent's garden are those of warmth and exuberance—along with a dramatic flair edging toward the outré. Coupled with the partners' sure taste in selecting plants with Mediterranean associations, the result is pure garden-theater magic, tucked away in a quiet Vancouver neighborhood.

CHECKLIST FOR GARDENING IN SMALL SPACES

- If you can "borrow" views of trees and large shrubs from the surrounding landscape, you will not have to give up valuable space in your garden for these large-scale elements. Techniques for borrowing include arranging lower shrubs and vegetation in your own garden to frame the desired view; arranging sitting areas in your garden to take advantage of the borrowed view; and coordinating the colors, textures, and shapes of plants in your garden to complement those in the borrowed view.

- Complement the colors and textures of your home in the foliage and blooms of the plants you select for the garden—this "marries" the house and garden to each other by creating visual flow between them.

- Use large planter boxes to contain varieties of trees and shrubs whose roots tolerate confined spaces without undue stress, including many varieties of pines, Japanese maples, bamboos, dogwoods, rhododendrons, camellias, and hydrangeas. (Such specimens will require more feeding and watering than they would if planted in open soil.)

- Use pots and planters to display bulbs, annuals, and perennials with interesting foliage and/or long flowering cycles. Consider adding a few pots of strictly foliage plants to your seasonal color displays in order to tone down the overall effect. Grasses, bergenias, hostas, hellebores, and ferns all take well to pot culture.

Above: A sunny terrace overflowing with plants in pots and with compact raised planting beds overlooks Vancouver's English Bay.

Left: The back alleys of most urban gardens tend to sport trash cans and clotheslines, but Thomas and Brent have created a shady walk planted with woodsy shrubs and groundcovers in theirs.

Opposite page: An ornate urn with a classical motif serves as the focal point of the small terrace garden.

- Winterize your potted plants by sinking them, pots and all, into a large mound of light soil and then covering them with a mulch of leaves, compost, or evergreen branches. Remember to water them during prolonged winter dry spells.

- Limit your plantings to favorite and choice varieties. (But don't limit your palette to dwarf, miniature, or otherwise tiny plants; this makes any garden space, even a constricted one, look bizarrely unnatural.)

- Consider eliminating turf from a small garden—it frees up space for more interesting plants, and lets you add visual richness to the garden floor with planted flagstones, bricks laid down in patterns, cobbled mosaics, and so on.

- Soften enclosing walls and fences with vines, espaliers, trellises, and wall-mounted fountains.

- Use cool colors for hardscapes and vegetation on the perimeters of a small garden in order to make its boundaries seem less obvious.

SMALL TREES FOR SMALL GARDENS

A well-known Chinese saying goes: "Marry if you want happiness for a week, but plant a tree if you want happiness for a lifetime." Planting trees is a pleasure that gardeners with small plots can indulge in only cautiously, since nothing imbalances a small lot quite so disastrously as too many trees. Even one really oversized tree, when its branches block the garden's light and air circulation and its roots monopolize the soil's moisture and nutrients, can be too much.

The trick here is to select a tree that has a strong personality yet remains compact enough not to crowd out the other plants in your garden. The trees described in the accompanying plant list either naturally grow no taller than 20 feet in most Northwest gardens or will tolerate the kind of long-term pruning that keeps them from growing larger. They also possess special qualities—such as graceful form interesting bark, or attractive foliage and blooms—that make them outstanding additions to the small garden.

SMALL TREES FOR SMALL GARDENS

Acer palmatum (many varieties)	Japanese maple	The Japanese name for these delicate maples means "tiny hands unfolding," and their leaves have a fluttering fragility that suits a small gardening space well. Their trunks become twisted and characterful as they age, adding a nice touch of maturity to the garden scene. Plant in moist, rich, well-drained soil, away from strong afternoon sun. *A. p.* 'Yugure' is especially choice; it grows slowly to a 7-to-13-foot-tall softly rounded tree, unfurls deeply lobed, scarlet leaves in spring that turn a deep rust in summer, and explodes into fresh crimson in fall.
Acer griseum	Paperbark maple	A small, spreading tree with outstanding presence year-round. The shaggy bark of this slow grower curls around the trunk in strips ranging from cinnamon-rust to glossy chestnut; the leaves turn scarlet in fall. Tolerates most normal growing conditions.
Albizia julibrissin	Silk tree	The graceful branches of this fast-growing spreader carry feathery light green leaves; pink powderpuff flowers in late summer freshen the garden when many other plants are looking dog-eared. Prune leader to keep the tree at 20 feet. Plant it in a sunny spot, and water it well.
Aralia elata	Japanese angelica tree	The showy compound leaves of this gently canopied spreader have a tropical luxuriance; white flower clusters float above the leaves in late summer. Plant this fast-growing tree in a sheltered corner, away from wind.
Cercis chinensis	Chinese redbud	Airy, multibranched, slow-growing tree with early, deep pink flowers and attractive shiny leaves that turn nicely in fall. Tolerates most normal growing conditions.
Cotinus coggygria 'Royal Purple'	Purple smoke tree	The delicate oval leaves of this fast-growing, rounded, multibranched tree turn several subtle variations of purple over the course of the growing season; smoky puffs of seed clusters last well into fall. Prefers poor soil and sunny exposures; drought-tolerant once established.

Continued on next page

SMALL TREES FOR SMALL GARDENS (cont.)

Hamamelis mollis	Chinese witch hazel	Hardy, pollution-tolerant, and taking either sun or shade, these small, slow-growing trees add the inestimable gift of fragrant, spidery blooms to the winter garden. Many varieties look coarse and gangly in youth, so be sure to prune them for shape from an early age; eventually they grow into handsome, stalwart little trees. *H. m.* 'Pallida' has deliciously soft canary-yellow blooms, while *H.* × *intermedia* 'Jelena' has dramatic gold-and-orange flowers.
Magnolia loebneri 'Dr. Merrill'		Grows outside our size limit, albeit slowly, to 25–30 feet, but has such handsome bark, branching patterns, and leaves that it's a worthy addition to the small garden. Lovely pure white flowers in midspring. Tolerates a range of growing conditions, but give it a good early start by enriching the planting hole with lots of compost and watering freely for the first few years.
Parrotia persica	Persian ironwood	A slow-growing mounder of wonderful year-round presence, with rough gray bark flaking to orange underlayers, and glossy, ribbed leaves turning brilliant rusts, golds, and scarlets in fall. Tolerates most growing conditions, but plant in full sun for best fall color.
Stewartia ovata		A beautifully proportioned, slow-growing tree with a compact habit, handsome bark, a white camellia-like flower in summer, and good fall coloring. A bit floppy-looking when young, but maturing to a mounding spreader. Plant it in rich, moist soil, away from strong afternoon sun, and water it well.

6

WATER GARDENS

URING MANY YEARS as a gardener-in-(self)training, I shied away from adding water features to my garden. Oh, I would read, from time to time, the motivating garden-speak on water being an essential garden element—about

Chinese designers calling it the "life's blood" of the garden, and how a central rectangular pool with four egressing *charbaghs* (water channels) configures every Islamic garden ever constructed in the last thousand years. And I would ponder, and had come to believe, Sir George Sitwell's dictum that "the magic of water . . . is ever the principal source of landscape beauty, and has, like music, a mysterious influence over the mind." But some equally mysterious influence seemed

to be stopping me from plunging into the installation of ponds, fountains, and streams in my own garden.

It took me a while to realize that influence was the emotion of fear. Not fear that I couldn't learn how to construct a water feature, or keep it functioning once it was installed. Rather, it was a fear of adding something to my garden so alive—so uncontrollable—as water.

For while it's true that you can't constrain plants either, the acts of planting, feeding, watering, and pruning them make gardeners feel like (benign) despots—able to gently shape landscapes and vegetation to their own requirements and desires.

But water is free, whether it runs in a stream, a pond, or a fountain. And it took me some time to feel comfortable enough with a certain quality in the garden which Mirabel Osler calls "gentle chaos" for the idea of adding water features to become truly appealing.

All gardeners follow different paths to their own, personal epiphanies—those moments of divine illumination that help them understand their roles in relationship to the landscapes they are creating. For me, the epiphany (or one of them—for, as with all engrossing avocations, they tend to keep happening) was realizing that I needn't dominate or control the landscape. And that by adding the anarchic element of water to my garden, I was inviting a dash of divine chaos into my soul at the same time.

❧ AN OLMSTED LEGACY IN THE NORTHWEST
Two Highlands Gardens
Seattle, Washington

As the designers of some of the Pacific Northwest's most notable public and private gardens during a period from the 1890s to the 1930s, the landscape architecture firm of the Olmsted Brothers has left an indelible mark on our region.

Its founder, Frederick Law Olmsted (1822–1903), began his career by designing such large-scale projects as New York's Central Park. By the period when most of its Pacific Northwest work was being done, Olmsted's sons and nephew were guiding the firm, but they had inherited his spacious, naturalistic approach to designing landscapes, as two Olmsted gardens preserved in Seattle's Highlands community demonstrate.

The Highlands itself is a 380-acre private planned community of 4- to 5-acre estates in northwest Seattle, overlooking Puget Sound. It was founded in 1907 by a group of prominent Seattle citizens, who later commissioned the Olmsted Brothers to plan the enclave's roads and open spaces. During the next 30 years the firm also designed gardens for many of The Highlands estates, and a few of those original gardens remain relatively intact today.

The signature elements of an Olmsted garden design include using natural contours in the landscape (or creating them when they are not there naturally), informally grouped stands of trees and shrubs, sweeping lawns, and elegantly framed views of far-off mountains, trees, water, or other significant landscape features.

This design approach obviously works best in a fairly spacious setting, and many Olmsted gardens in The Highlands possess the atmosphere of handsome, dignified, and exquisitely well maintained parks. In order to give these parklands a more personal, intimate character—in other words, to make them into gardens rather than simply estate "grounds"—the firm added carefully designed garden features, among them pools, ponds, and streams.

A Highlands garden designed by the Olmsted Brothers in the late 1920s and now owned by Colleen and Kevin Stamper shows how water features can be used to help define various garden areas and to provide each with its own character.

The most formal area of the garden, encompassing about an acre, centers on a long lawn that sweeps down and away from the house, with its edges planted with mature conifers, rhododendrons, dogwoods, and flowering cherries. Several water features in this area underscore its quietly classic elegance, such as a lion's-head wall fountain flanked by espaliered fruit trees on a stone-flagged terrace adjoining the house, and a narrow, 70-foot-long water channel designed to collect and hold water seeping down from wooded hills above it. The channel originally gravity-fed its excess runoff to an artificial pond situated below it. This pond's oval concrete rim meets the clipped turf around it with a sharply formal edge. (Efforts are currently under way to repair the water channel and to renovate other timeworn

A "secret garden" in the Colleen and Kevin Stamper garden in The Highlands, near Seattle, centers on a round reflecting pool. A circular arbor covered in wisteria extends the lines of the pool toward the sky.

features of the original Olmsted plan—a most welcome act of regional garden preservation.)

Beyond the formal lawn lies a "secret garden" enclosed by hedges, whose romantic, intimate atmosphere contrasts with the spacious lawn area outside. Although this secret garden is small and lush, its central focus—a round concrete pond encircled by a wisteria-bearing trellis—echoes the formality of the water features belonging to the larger garden, albeit on a smaller scale. The ponds in each of these garden rooms employ water as a reflective surface material that also outlines the formal geometry of their shapes.

Water is used in the same capacity in another Highlands garden, where an intricately configured pond gives definition and shape to an otherwise anonymous stretch of turf. The formality of this pool's design is enhanced by the clipped evergreens in stone urns sited at each corner.

In both of these gardens the Olmsted-designed ponds are scaled appropriately to the surrounding landscape, and they are shallow enough to make the sheets of water they contain calm, reflective, and decorative, in keeping with the atmosphere of that landscape. One might compare them to cloudy old mirrors hanging on the walls of eighteenth century drawing rooms—they add further polish and refinement to an already exquisitely conceived and executed formal setting.

In another, less formal, part of the Stamper garden, water features are used to play up the naturally hilly terrain and lush vegetation. A wide, shallow stream half choked with

Above: This formal pool gives character and focus to a stretch of lawn in another Olmsted-designed garden in The Highlands.
Below: A formal wall fountain complements the geometric lines of the paths and planting beds on a terrace adjoining the Stamper residence.

iris and primulas winds through a narrow ravine to a roughly textured stone bridge, which is almost engulfed by a shaggy climbing hydrangea; the banks of a nearby naturally contoured pond disappear in a tangle of mosses, groundcovers, and rushes. Both stream and pond have been designed and planted to underscore the naturalistic "wildness" that characterizes this area of the garden, helping to distinguish it from the more formal areas closer to the house.

The Olmsted Brothers understood how to use water features to bring out the most essential design qualities in a landscape, from formal, limpid pools carved into stretches of carefully clipped turf to meandering streams that hug the curves and contours of a "wild" hill or ravine. Our region is fortunate that some of their gardens still remain, both as beautiful creations in their own right and as sources of inspiration for coming generations of our gardeners.

❧ A DEEP, DARK HEART
Arthur Erickson's Garden
Vancouver, British Columbia

If The Highlands' gardens illustrate how water can be used as a decorative design element on the surface of the landscape, Arthur Erickson's garden in Vancouver, British Columbia, shows how water can serve as a landscape's central focus—and in the process become its deep, dark heart.

Erickson, the internationally renowned architect whose work includes Vancouver's Robson Square Law Courts and the campus of Simon Fraser University, moved onto a small urban lot on the city's west side in 1957. At that time the 65- by 120-foot property featured a Tudor-style cottage surrounded by fruit trees, perennial borders, and beds of vegetables. Although he had never gardened before moving in, Arthur was excited at the prospect of keeping up and expanding the original garden.

With hindsight, Arthur now says that he had no idea of the amount of time it takes to maintain such a garden, and

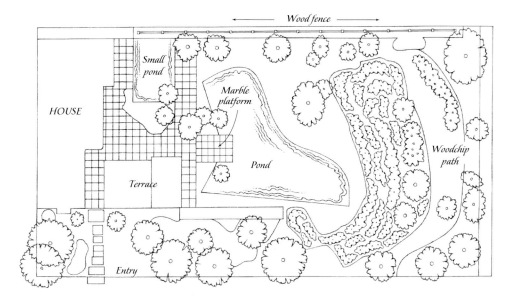

Above: Arthur Erickson's garden

consequently he didn't do much at all the first year. "By the second year it was looking charmingly wild, but by the third year it was simply a mess. I decided to pull out the lawns and vegetables and to put in a garden that would take care of itself, where the plants could run wild and still look good."

As a first step, he built a gentle mound of earth toward the south end of the lot, in order to block out a row of houses on the next street. The large hole left in front of the mound he made into a pond.

Because of its location in the center of the garden, the pond dominates the landscape. With its dark fingers reaching into the bamboos, groundcovers, and rushes that rim it, the pond has a rather mesmerizing presence, drawing a visitor's attention downward into its still, dark waters. Rather than serving as a reflective surface, as in the Olmsted ponds, the water in Erickson's pond brings depth, mystery, and concentrated power to the garden landscape.

In keeping with Arthur's hands-off philosophy of gardening, the pond is self-regulating: a naturally arrived at balance of fish, aquatic plants, snails, and frogs keeps the waters clean and mosquito-free. The 40-year-old tarpaper

The still pond that serves as the heart of Arthur Erickson's Vancouver garden.

liner has started to leak a little in recent years, Arthur says, but beyond topping up the water level occasionally in summer, he does no maintenance.

"This garden, and especially the pond, are about as close as you can get, in an artificial situation, to a landscape at peace with itself. It feels as though it's hardly been invaded by humans at all," Arthur says.

The plants he chose to site around the pond's edges, such as lush stands of ornamental grasses, mahonias, and native ferns, also contribute to its atmosphere of wild serenity. Many of the trees and plants in the garden arrived naturally, as seeds planted by birds. Although wild-growing plants with relaxed habits dominate the garden, structural touches throughout, such as clipped azaleas and Japanese hollies, keep the landscape from looking formless.

Several hardscapes also play a role in creating the garden's atmosphere of minimalist elegance. A tall cedar fence encloses the entire lot, and Arthur cleverly staggered some of the boards about a foot behind the rest of the fence, so that ferns and bamboos planted in the freed-up spaces could spill out to soften the garden perimeters.

A square marble platform juts out into the pond from the side of the house, introducing one of the few formal shapes into the landscape. Its severe lines are mirrored, and thereby balanced, by a nearby Japanese holly, clipped to a similar size and shape. (Legend has it that Rudolf Nureyev danced on the platform one night during an Erickson party—surely an act of courage as well as of creative imagination, since the slippery marble surface tips toward the pond at a slight but disorienting angle.)

Efforts are currently under way to preserve Arthur Erickson's house and garden as a Canadian cultural heritage property, with the aim of eventually opening the garden to

Above: Bamboo, ferns, and mahonias soften the staggered base of a fence constructed near the edge of the pond.

Below: Once Erickson had designed, constructed, and planted it, he left his pond alone "to evolve according to its own nature." Forty years later, goldfish, raccoons, and a variety of waterfowl call it home.

the public. Meanwhile, Arthur strolls the garden almost every morning, watching the way the light from the sky falls on the pond, absorbing the latest depredations of the neighboring raccoons (whose favorite nighttime prank is uprooting outdoor lighting fixtures and throwing them into the pond), and counting the birds visiting the bamboo thickets that crown the garden's mound.

He says the pond remains fascinating after almost 40 years because "it shows me something new every day." A visitor comes away wondering, too, whether the pond serves an inspirational role in Erickson's creative life—in much the same way that it serves as his garden's hypnotic center for life, light, energy, and power.

✿ MAGIC WATERS
David Lewis's and George Little's Garden
Bainbridge Island, Washington

The water features in the Olmsted gardens and the Erickson garden were designed to underscore and enhance the qualities of the landscapes surrounding them. But does the Pacific Northwest have room for an entirely different approach for using water features—one that establishes its own unique style through the intensive use of exotic plants and dramatic hardscapes, so that it would look just as much at home in a villa in a Mediterranean port city or in a jungle garden on the equator as it does here in our own region?

David Lewis and George Little have created such a water garden on Puget Sound's Bainbridge Island. I first saw it as I was traveling down a bystreet, lost on the way to a ferry. Even driving by at 30 mph and with a pressing desire to catch the next ferry uppermost on my mind, I instinctively pulled the car off the road, and approached the lot on foot, with all my "Oooooh—this looks like a good garden!!!" antennae quivering.

David and George were not at home, but a friend who was caretaking the garden for them permitted us to roam the grounds freely. It was an exciting walkabout, principally because we kept encountering hardscapes— fountains, columns, wall plaques, and ponds—that had shapes, textures, and colors seldom seen in traditional Northwest gardens.

The pieces of garden art combine a contemporary sense of whimsy with the timelessly monumental look of Greek, Roman, Egyptian, and Mayan architecture. Made mostly of poured concrete stained or painted in exuberant Mediterranean and tropical aquamarines, roses, and ochres, they are meant to have, says David Lewis, "an excavated look, like they've been on the site for a millennium."

Meeting David and George on a later visit, I learned where their artistic inspiration came from. David trained in classical studies at Oberlin College and spent several years in Greece working on archaeological digs. When he moved to Bainbridge Island in 1988, David bought a rambler on a modest-sized lot that was adorned with the usual lawn and foundation plants. During the next four years he incorporated into the garden design the vision of a maze of small rooms outlined in stone. Using brick and stone, he constructed rectangular pools and planting beds that carved the lawn into a series of interlocking garden rooms and spaces. These patterns resemble, from a bird's-eye view, the excavated ruins of an ancient Greek house, with its atriums, colonnades, and courtyard gardens.

After David met sculptor George Little in 1992, they began a creative collaboration by adding George's sculptures and fountains to the garden. George, a sculptor with 25 years of experience in making artwork for public spaces, has been fascinated from youth with the heavy, powerful lines of Minoan, Middle Eastern, and Mesoamerican architecture. He also admires the playful spirit and daring colors of Mexican folk art.

When he met David, George was inspired to start combining his sculptures with plants and water in outdoor settings. The partners fashion their original pieces in plaster and clay, prepare molds from them, and then pour concrete

into the molds. During this process, they take special care
to preserve the concrete's rough texture; the resulting time-
worn, gently eroded surfaces make the pieces look like
sculptures from a lost civilization.

Their signature pieces may be the columns—squatter
and more dynamic than the classical Greek and Roman
ones—that adorn the garden pools. These columns have
water pipes fitted through their cores so that water can
slide down their mossy outside surfaces. Shallow basins
carved into the the tops of the columns cradle exotic
grasses and water plants. Together, the columns, water,
and plants conjure Mayan ruins slowly crumbling under
jungle vegetation.

George and David use water in their artwork most
notably as a quicksilver, purling, murmuring medium that
contrasts with the monumental immutability of their

columns and fountains. Along with the vibrant colors and dynamic forms of the hardscapes, this contrast between two essential elements adds drama to the whole garden.

Which, David explains, is exactly the atmosphere the partners wanted to create: "We want to keep the theatrics out, but at the same time we want a visitor to stand back in awe, to find elements of mystery and discovery here."

Surely the Pacific Northwest, even with its traditional emphasis on understated and naturalistic garden design, is ready to welcome the bold new approach to water features that George Little and David Lewis bring to their Bainbridge Island garden. By incorporating the motifs and symbols of ancient and exotic civilizations into their garden art, they enrich the repertoire of metaphors and allusions from which the rest of us, as gardeners, can draw as we decorate the regional landscape.

POCKET-SIZED PONDS

For those with limited gardening space, a container can become a miniature water habitat, complete with plants, fish, and scavengers. Here are some guidelines for creating these rich, but surprisingly easy to maintain, environments:

1. Use a waterproof container at least 18 inches deep that holds 30 gallons or more of water. (For a handy comparison, a whiskey half-barrel—at 18 inches deep and 24 inches in diameter—holds 32 gallons.)

2. Site the container where it will receive four to five hours of sun a day, but not in a spot so hot at midday that the water heats up appreciably. (Fish and plants can be harmed by excessively warm water.)

3. Choose a variety of water plants with which to stock your container. Each plant type performs a different role in creating a healthy environment:

   • Oxygenators are submerged plants that add oxygen to the water to keep it clean and clear. They should take up no more than a third of the container's underwater volume.

PLANTS FOR A WATER GARDEN

OXYGENATORS

Hottonia palustris (water violet), *Lemna minor* (common duckweed), *Myriophyllum aquaticum* (parrot's feather), *Ranunculus aquatilis* (water crowfoot)

SURFACE PLANTS/FLOATING PLANTS

Aponogeton distachyus (water hawthorn), *Cyperus alternifolius* (umbrella grass), *Eichhornia crassipes* (water hyacinth), *Hydrocharis morsus-ranae* (frogbit), *Nymphaea* spp. (water lilies), *Pistia stratiotes* (water lettuce)

MARGINALS

Acorus calamus (sweet flag), *Calla palustris* (bog arum), *Caltha palustris* (marsh marigold), *Equisetum hyemale* (horsetail), *Iris pseudiacorus* (yellow flag), *Pontederia cordata* (pickerel weed), *Sagittaria japonica* (arrowhead plant)

- Surface plants keep their roots submerged while their leaves and flowers float on the water's surface. Floating plants keep both roots and leaves on the surface of the water. Both surface plants and floating plants shade the water, keeping it cool and shady for fish and preventing the growth of algae.

- Marginals, such as iris and some grasses, like to keep their roots in shallow water or boggy soil; they are used to extend the plant palette with which you can decorate the edges of a waterscape. If your container is deep, you can elevate a potted marginal on submerged bricks so that its roots are close to the surface.

4. For a container holding approximately 32 gallons of water, add two or three generous bunches of oxygenators, two surface plants, and enough floating plants and marginals to cover 60 to 70 percent of the water's surface.

5. When adding surface and marginal plants to your container, cover the surface of the pots they are planted in with gravel; this will keep the water clear of excess floating dirt when you submerge the pots.

6. After two or three days, add two goldfish (same sex!) and several water snails for cleaning the sides and bottom of the container.

7. Feed the fish sparingly (they should be able to scavenge a lot of their diet from the organic plant debris that naturally appears in the water), and fertilize the plants with a stingy hand. Both fish food and fertilizer add excess nutrients to the water that can upset the natural balance you are aiming for.

Right: Concrete columns topped by baskets filled with moisture-loving iris and Equisetum *dominate the skyline of the Bainbridge Island, Washington, garden of David Lewis and George Little.*

Opposite page: Clay, ceramic, and concrete containers create miniature waterscapes within the boundaries of a larger pool.

Checklist of Design Considerations for Siting a Pond in Your Garden

- Locate the pond in an easily accessible spot near paths, preferably with a comfortable viewing area adjoining it. The pond also should be located near sources of water (for topping up) and of electricity (for running pumps and outdoor lighting).

- Plan to make your pond as large as the site can reasonably support; an expansive sheet of water looks infinitely more alluring than a puddle.

- Site the pond in a low spot in your garden to replicate the way that water collects and settles in the natural landscape.

- Construct the pond on freely draining soil or a gravel foundation. Unstable soil can crack the pond liner or cause its sides to cave in. Also plan to install an overflow drain on the edge of your pond if the site will be subject to flooding once the pond is built.

- Site the pond where no herbicides, pesticides, or oily runoff from roads will wash into it.

- Site the pond where it will receive five to eight hours of sunlight a day if you plan to stock it with fish, water lilies, and other sun-loving plants.

- A pond that is to be stocked with fish and aquatic plants should have at least 50 square feet of surface area and should also be at least 18 inches deep. Ponds smaller than this experience too much fluctuation in water temperature for the health of fish and plants.

- Locate your pond away from overhanging deciduous trees and shrubs, unless you plan to clear the water of leaves and other debris on a regular basis. Decaying organic material can cloud water, harm fish, and damage filters and pumps.

- Building codes sometimes require that ponds deeper than 3 feet have fences built around them. Consult your local building department for further information.

CHAPTER

7

GARDENING ON A SLOPE

Much of the maritime Pacific Northwest lies on hilly terrain. If we were to examine the region on a raised contour map, it would show jagged, snowy mountain crags gradually sloping down to the Pacific

Ocean, with steep green valleys snaking between the mountains' foothills to narrow, twisting rivers that eventually feed into lakes. Because so much of our topography is composed of this westward slide toward the ocean, many Northwesterners find themselves dealing with the pleasures and pains of gardening on hills and slopes.

The pleasures are many: nothing adds quite so much drama and mystery to a garden as paths that crawl up, down, and around ravines and hillsides, while

the opportunity to weave trees, shrubs, groundcovers, and vines together on a three-dimensional grid—paying attention to width, depth, *and* height—enriches a landscape's design potential exponentially.

Sharp changes in elevation also allow us to view plants from novel perspectives. When looked down on from above, for example, the softly rounded crowns of silk trees *(Albizia julibrissin)* and the feathery seed heads of tall ornamental grasses such as *Miscanthus sinensis* take on a new beauty,

one we can't appreciate from our normal viewpoint. On the other hand, the 2-foot-tall Solomon's seal *(Polygonatum),* with its arching leaves and drooping flower bells, looks modest, charming, and woodsy when viewed from above, but it becomes transformed into a quite sinister and rampant jungle "vine" when you find yourself staring up at it from below.

Hardscapes also play a role in the sloping garden. Boulders and stones, as well as water features such as streams and waterfalls, achieve some their best effects when steeply vertical terrain forms their backdrops. A flight of stairs can add formal drama to a hillside, while a simple garden chair or bench placed near a far-ranging view can finish off, and perfect, its crowning point.

But numerous problems plague the sloping garden. Controlling erosion and protecting from wind, dealing with drainage, amending soil, the planting, fertilizing, weeding, and watering of vegetation—all of these practical garden tasks can seem especially onerous when you undertake them on a hillside. Although this book remains focused on design solutions to landscaping problems, the three gardens presented in this chapter also demonstrate some practical techniques and approaches that any gardener who has a sloping yard, and who is equipped with a shovel and a wheelbarrow, will find of use.

Above: Fifty-year-old retaining walls, built of a local granite, lead to the main garden rooms of Andrew Yeomans's and Noël Richardson's Ravenhill Herb Farm on Vancouver Island.

Opposite top: A formal garden room cut into a slope forms the heart of Ravenhill Herb Farm.

Opposite bottom: Low stone steps lead to the formal garden room, which is planted in herbs and colorful annuals.

❀ RAVENHILL'S ROOM WITH A VIEW

Andrew Yeomans's and Noël Richardson's Garden
Vancouver Island, British Columbia

In 1978 Andrew Yeomans and Noël Richardson decided to leave their hectic city lives behind and find a country place in which to garden, raise sheep, and tend bees. Their search centered on the northern end of Vancouver Island, where they eventually found a 10-acre sloping property that came complete with a fine old house, a series of stone walls, and the remains of several ancient tennis courts.

Andrew and Noël found the property, which they named Ravenhill Herb Farm, especially enticing because it featured an extensive south-facing slope with superb natural drainage. Andrew, a gardener, and Noël, a cook specializing in dishes using culinary herbs, planned to grow herbs on a commercial basis to support their new way of life in the country, and they thought the slope would provide just the right conditions for growing their cash crop.

Andrew says that when they first acquired the property, "the garden had some bulbs and lawns, but few other interesting plants, while the house was so poorly sited relative to the hillside that it looked like it might tumble down it. Nothing was wrong structurally, it just *looked* precarious."

Ravenhill's Room with a View

Andrew Yeomans's and Noël Richardson's Garden
Vancouver Island, British Columbia

GARDEN SITE	*A country garden overlooking a valley on north Vancouver Island*
TOPOGRAPHY	*A level, rectangular garden room, 60 ft. long by 30 ft. wide, cut into a steeply graded south-facing slope*
SOIL	*Free-draining, slightly heavy soil that is amended with 3 in. of leaf mold every year*
LIGHT	*The south side of the garden is shady a good part of the day; the north side receives full sun all day*
AVERAGE ANNUAL RAINFALL	*33.9 in.*
AVERAGE MINIMUM TEMPERATURE	*37° F (2.8° C), with strong southwest winds raking the hillside during late fall and early winter*
MAINTENANCE	*Several days of cleanup and mulching in late winter; 1 to 2 hours per week of tidying during the growing season*

Andrew decided to create a garden around the house that would solve several problems—both aesthetic and practical ones—at the same time. "I wanted to establish broad, horizontal planes beside and below the house, so that it would feel stabilized, like it was part of the slope. At the same time, I wanted to use the wonderful growing conditions on the slope for planting herbs," he explains. "Today, the garden is a series of interlocking horizontal planes on several different levels; now, wherever you look out from the house, you feel firmly connected to the various garden rooms that we've established below and beside it."

Perhaps the most eye-catching of these "stabilizing" garden rooms lies below the house on a level rectangular terrace 60 feet long by 30 feet wide. It features formal planting beds, filled with herbs, that are set into brick pavers. This garden is enclosed on one end by a low mortared stone wall and on the other end by a greenhouse. With its large terra-cotta pots filled with clipped herbs, and a silvered wooden bench set exactly parallel to one axis of the geometric beds, the garden possesses a kind of countrified formality that blends with the surrounding landscape while at the same time giving it shape and definition.

Andrew says that they didn't have to do much earth-moving at all to establish this and the other garden rooms, in part because the tennis court ruins already provided them with significant stretches of leveled land. But they did add some low retaining walls at especially steep points in the garden, primarily because they were able to secure the same local granite (from a quarry located half a mile away) from which the property's original stone walls had been built in the 1930s. These walls both continue and extend the formal style for hardscapes that Andrew established in the herb garden, while also visually tying together old and new parts of the garden.

Andrew chose to create a formal room for his herb garden because "plants, especially herbs, tend to have softly rounded shapes, with fuzzy edges. Their main design problem is how to show off this look to best effect. I find

Above: Landscape architect Hoichi Kurisu created a "mountain of rock" as the focal point of David and Elaine Frey's garden in Lake Oswego, Oregon.

Opposite page: A stream links the Freys' house and its adjoining rock feature to a hot tub and swimming pool sited below.

that using the hard edges of pavers and stone near the planting beds makes for strong visual contrasts— soft on hard—which makes a garden look more interesting."

The formal approach works not only within the boundaries of the herb garden itself but also as a way to integrate the garden room into the larger landscape: its strong horizontal plane echoes the wide east-to-west sweep of the valley below it. The entire scene brings to mind the more gentle and settled portions of the countryside of northern Italy and Switzerland, where cultivated slopes and fields stretch into a horizon filled with deep mountain lakes and forested hillsides.

❧ AN ERUPTION OF ROCK
David and Elaine Frey's Garden
Lake Oswego, Oregon

Many Northwesterners who are building new houses are careful to site them in ways that will take advantage of a potential view. But sometimes this makes for a complicated interface between the house and its grounds, as David and Elaine Frey discovered when they built their new home on a steep bank overlooking the Willamette River.

When the Freys commissioned landscape architect Hoichi Kurisu to design and install a garden on the site, they asked for a plan that would include sweeping views from all the rooms of the house that look toward the river, an outside hot tub and a swimming pool, some Northwest native plantings, and a large level stretch of lawn near the banks of the river.

The space Kurisu had in which to accomplish this work was rather small and awkwardly configured. It was a

An Eruption of Rock

David and Elaine Frey's Garden
Lake Oswego, Oregon

GARDEN SITE	*A suburban estate overlooking the Willamette River*
TOPOGRAPHY	*A rectangular garden 32 ft. deep by 50 ft. wide, with a northern exposure; a steep "hill" of boulders slopes down and away from the house toward a large level lawn adjoining the riverbank*
SOIL	*Originally a sandbank; soil has been thoroughly amended*
LIGHT	*Full sun for approximately 80 percent of the day*
AVERAGE ANNUAL RAINFALL	*39.4 in.*
AVERAGE MINIMUM TEMPERATURE	*39° F (3.9° C)*
MAINTENANCE	*Low*

steep slope approximately 32 feet long, running down and away from the house toward the riverbank, with a vertical drop of 12 feet. In this area Kurisu had to create enough level space to construct the hot tub and swimming pool, while at the same time absorbing the 12-foot drop between house and riverside in a way that permitted easy and convenient circulation between the two planes.

Kurisu studied landscape architecture in his native Japan before moving to Portland in the 1960s to assume directorship of the Portland Japanese Garden. He has been in private practice now for over 20 years, and in the intervening period has developed a special love for working with rock. Today many of his garden plans feature dramatic stonescapes, usually ones designed to serve several functional and aesthetic purposes at the same time.

In the Frey garden Hoichi elected to site a massive rock arrangement—150 tons of gray Oregon basalt—next to the house, because it solved several problems simultaneously. Practically, the rockery accommodates the deep vertical drop within a relatively short distance, while also uniting the house and level garden areas with several wide, shallow flights of steps.

Aesthetically, the rock arrangement ties the house to the riverside, which uses the same large basalt boulders to stabilize its banks, and to the rest of the garden, which features basalt stepping stones and paths throughout. The rockery also acts as a pleasingly informal "planter" for some

Northwest native plants that won't grow tall enough to obstruct the view, among them vine maples *(Acer circinatum)*, Oregon grape *(Mahonia aquifolium)*, and salal *(Gaultheria shallon)*.

As a finishing touch, Hoichi created a stream that flows through the rock arrangement, so that the element of water would serve as a common, connecting thread between the house, the pools, and the riverside.

In essence, the rock arrangement functions in the Frey garden as a retaining wall. But instead of creating a sheer and looming 12-foot-high barrier, Hoichi designed the rockwork to act as the visual focal point of the garden, complete with softening plants and an attractive water feature. The fact that this rock feature gives the garden, at the same time, a unique identity or character that it would not otherwise possess is a bonus—the kind of bonus likely to occur when a designer uses skill and ingenuity of a high order to solve a landscaping problem common to many Northwest gardens.

✿ ALONG A HILLSIDE PATH
Margaret Lockett's Garden
Issaquah, Washington

The two previous examples in this chapter showed us two ways in which you can alter the grade in order to integrate a garden with the slope it rests upon. Margaret Lockett's garden shows us another, completely different, approach: leave your hillside essentially unaltered, and adapt your hardscapes and planting style to what is already there.

When Margaret Lockett and her late husband built their house on view property overlooking Lake Sammamish in 1984, their backyard was a narrow, rectangular lot tumbling down a hillside that was covered in blackberry vines and stinging nettles.

Margaret had gardened at a previous home for 20 years, "so I had already made my mistakes there, and I knew what I wanted for my new garden." But her new

Above: Margaret Lockett's Issaquah, Washington, garden sits on a steep slope overlooking Lake Sammamish.

Opposite page: The view going up Margaret's garden is created by wide, informally planted beds that stretch across the narrow, steep lot.

plans were subject to several restrictions. She could not impede the views of neighbors by planting tall trees; retaining walls and terraces were outside the limits of the garden budget; her husband didn't want to install a lawn that he would then be responsible for mowing; and—because she planned to do most of the gardening herself—Margaret, who was in her mid-60s at the time, restricted her palette to plants "that I could handle by myself—nothing very big or difficult."

Within these parameters, Margaret set out to "plant the things I like—lots of Mediterranean plants, grasses with blue-gray leaves, and foliage plants with gray leaves. I also like Japanese maples and woodland plants."

After clearing the slope of weeds and amending the soil, Margaret established several growing areas, each featuring a

Along a Hillside Path

Margaret Lockett's Garden
Issaquah, Washington

GARDEN SITE	*A suburban lot high on a hill overlooking Lake Sammamish*
TOPOGRAPHY	*A narrow, rectangular garden, 70 ft. wide by 300 ft. long, on a northwest-facing slope; altitude is approximately 600 feet*
SOIL	*Glacial till, covered in several inches of rich humus, with excellent natural drainage; amendments include removal of small stones and the addition of sawdust and cow manure; compost is occasionally spread on heavy feeders*
LIGHT	*Full sun most of the day, although the garden area immediately in the lee of the house loses sun by midafternoon*
AVERAGE ANNUAL RAINFALL	*39.9 in.*
AVERAGE MINIMUM TEMPERATURE	*38° F (3.3° C); the garden is sheltered from winter winds by nearby Cougar Mountain, which lies to the southwest; there are no frost pockets because of excellent drainage and air movement*
MAINTENANCE	*One full day of maintenance every two weeks; occasional sessions of tidying up in between during the growing season*

different garden style and plant palette. These areas are informally grouped and shade into one another with soft, blurry edges.

At the bottom of the garden lot is a "woodlands room," where Margaret's collection of Japanese maples can grow to their full size without obstructing anyone's view. This woodlands area also blends the bottom edge of the garden into the woodsy natural landscape that surrounds it.

Partway up the slope, where the topography is steepest and the sun at its most powerful, there is a decidedly Mediterranean feel to the garden. A gravel path meanders from side to side of the lot, separated from the naturally contoured planting beds by small edging stones, whose gray tones echo the colors of the house and gravel and also provide a nice backdrop to the gray, blue-green, and silver foliage of the plants. Here Margaret has grouped her lavenders, roses, artemisias, ornamental grasses, sunroses *(Helianthemum spp.)*, and small naturalizing bulbs.

Closer to the house, where the plants receive some protection from full sun, she returns to a woodlands theme by planting ferns, small rhododendrons, primroses, and other lovers of high shade.

The design rationale behind Margaret's garden plan is simplicity itself. Using the natural contours of the slope, she has established informal planting beds that flow down the hillside in wide swaths. Each bed is filled with the types of plants best suited to its particular microclimate, with attention paid to layering plants according to height and shape. The wandering gravel path connects the various planting beds, providing visual continuity, easy access to all parts of the garden, and handy viewing points for looking at the sweep of hill and lake below.

The eminent garden designer Russell Page once observed that "gardens falling away from the house are seldom much visited." I suppose he meant that such gardens don't feel comfortable to visitors, in part because we are always assessing whether the quick journey down will be worth the long toil back up. But when the design is so elegantly understated and the beds are so intriguingly planted as in Margaret Lockett's garden, I'm sure that even Mr. Page would have felt a stroll down its path was well worth the return climb.

CHECKLIST FOR GARDENING ON SLOPES

- Respect, as far as possible, the natural contours of the land: amend and enhance the original grade rather than completely altering it.

- Create numerous wide, shallow terraces on a slope rather than a few steep ones. This approach works both aesthetically—the garden looks stable and inviting—and practically—the problems of soil and water erosion are less acute.

- In extremely steep areas where regrading is not an option, use the vertical drop as a dramatic design feature by installing a rock outcropping, a waterfall, or an eye-catching, low-maintenance shrub or groundcover. Take the trouble to address this design problem head-on at the beginning, because if you don't deal with it now, it will be much more difficult to amend later on,

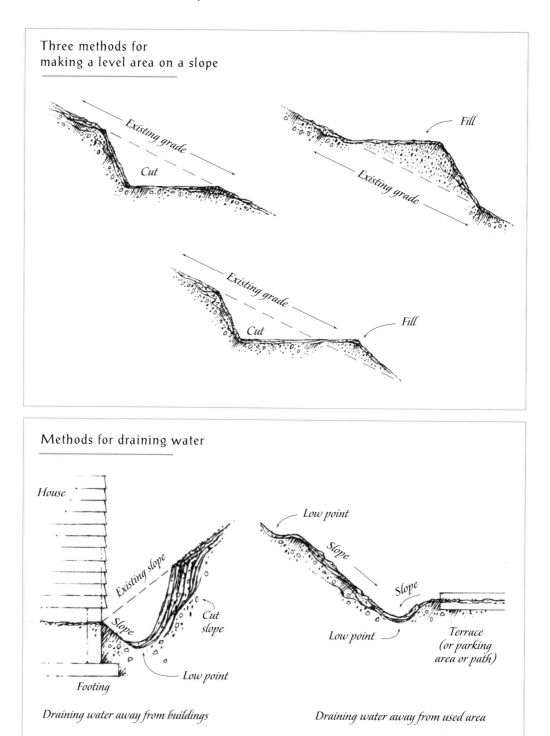

Three methods for
making a level area on a slope

Existing grade

Cut

Fill

Existing grade

Existing grade

Cut

Fill

Methods for draining water

House

Existing slope

Slope

Cut
slope

Low point

Footing

Draining water away from buildings

Low point

Slope

Slope

Low point

Terrace
(or parking
area or path)

Draining water away from used area

once the surrounding area is nicely settled in with plants. (Does this sound like the voice of experience?)

• Maintain continuity among the styles and materials you use for hillside hardscapes. For example, if you construct a low retaining "baffle" of uncut stone as the edging for an informal terrace, use similarly informal kinds of stone, such as gravel or rough stepping stones, for the paths and steps nearby. On the other hand, formal terraces built with flagstone or brick require that nearby retaining walls, steps, and paths be made of cut stone or mortared brick.

• When constructing a path, make sure that the grade and the surface material allow you to move a wheelbarrow up and down its length. When constructing a flight of steps, install a ramp alongside them for moving a wheelbarrow. (If this is not practical, you can lay a board over the steps temporarily while moving the wheelbarrow.)

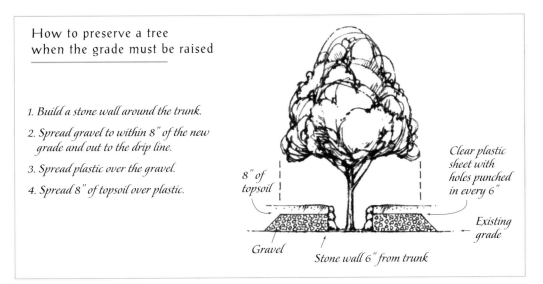

How to preserve a tree
when the grade must be raised

1. *Build a stone wall around the trunk.*

2. *Spread gravel to within 8" of the new grade and out to the drip line.*

3. *Spread plastic over the gravel.*

4. *Spread 8" of topsoil over plastic.*

8" of topsoil

Clear plastic sheet with holes punched in every 6"

Existing grade

Gravel

Stone wall 6" from trunk

• On hillsides to be planted, remove all weeds and weed roots from the original soil. This time-consuming step is vital for retaining your sanity in subsequent growing seasons—having to weed on a steep slope year after year

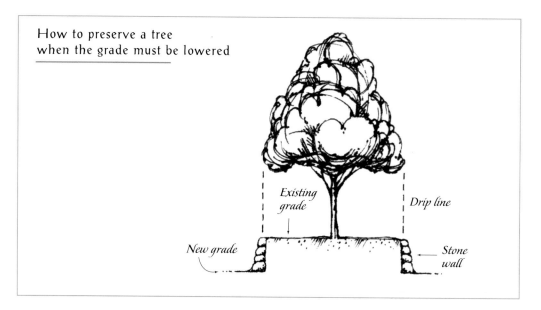

How to preserve a tree
when the grade must be lowered

Existing grade

Drip line

New grade

Stone wall

is one of my personal definitions of cruel and preventable punishment.

• Amend the soil to be planted deeply and richly; a good, healthy soil inhibits erosion by absorbing water and nutrients quickly, thereby encouraging soil-binding root growth.

• If you plan to use waterwise plants on your hillside (as suggested on page 159), you can install an efficient, inexpensive temporary watering system by snaking

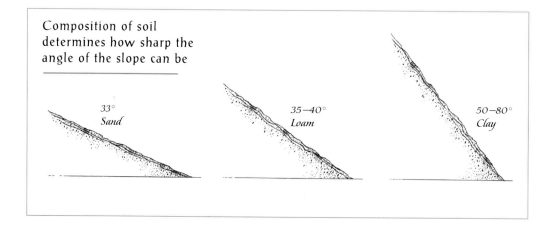

Composition of soil
determines how sharp the
angle of the slope can be

33°
Sand

35–40°
Loam

50–80°
Clay

rubber soaker hoses across the slope in broad horizontal swaths and then burying them 2 or 3 inches below the surface with a spade. The hoses will disintegrate underground within two to four years, at just about the time that the roots of your newly established plants are becoming able to fend for themselves.

- On very steep slopes, cover the amended ground with a retaining cloth made of natural fibers, such as coconut, jute, or cotton, before beginning to plant. These retaining cloths will prevent erosion for the first year or two, while the roots of the newly established plants are becoming firmly entrenched. The natural fiber cloths will disintegrate within several years, adding more organic material to the soil.

- Plant your hillside with low-maintenance, waterwise trees, shrubs, and perennials, and then underplant these with bulbs that naturalize and with weed-suppressing groundcovers. (See page 159 for a sample planting.) After planting, mulch the area heavily for weed suppression, moisture retention, and erosion control.

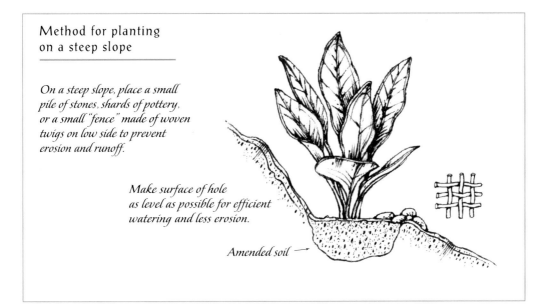

Method for planting on a steep slope

On a steep slope, place a small pile of stones, shards of pottery, or a small "fence" made of woven twigs on low side to prevent erosion and runoff.

Make surface of hole as level as possible for efficient watering and less erosion.

Amended soil →

Trouble spots on a slope

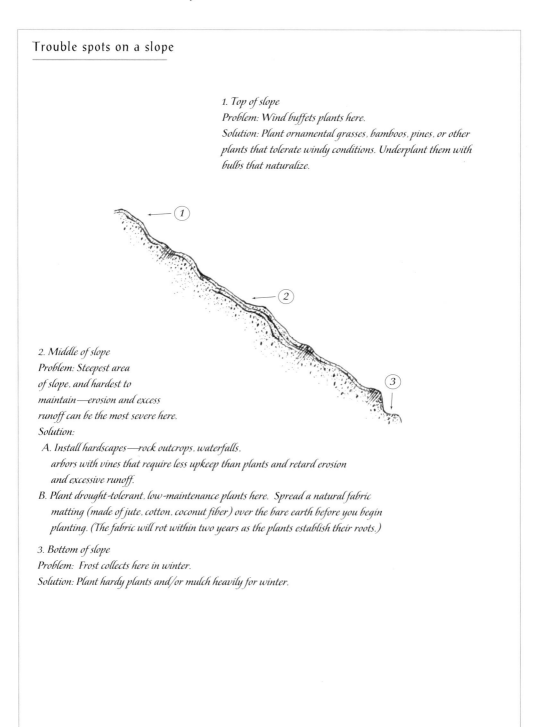

1. Top of slope
Problem: Wind buffets plants here.
Solution: Plant ornamental grasses, bamboos, pines, or other
plants that tolerate windy conditions. Underplant them with
bulbs that naturalize.

2. Middle of slope
Problem: Steepest area
of slope, and hardest to
maintain—erosion and excess
runoff can be the most severe here.
Solution:
  A. Install hardscapes—rock outcrops, waterfalls,
     arbors with vines that require less upkeep than plants and retard erosion
     and excessive runoff.
  B. Plant drought-tolerant, low-maintenance plants here. Spread a natural fabric
     matting (made of jute, cotton, coconut fiber) over the bare earth before you begin
     planting. (The fabric will rot within two years as the plants establish their roots.)

3. Bottom of slope
Problem: Frost collects here in winter.
Solution: Plant hardy plants and/or mulch heavily for winter.

A Sample Planting for a South-Facing Hillside with a 35-Degree Slope

This planting scheme plays off the basic color combinations of dusty greens, blue greens, purples, and silvers for foliage, and whites and pinks for blooms. It will fill an area approximately 9 feet deep by 18 feet wide. The plants have been selected as waterwise and low-maintenance.

TREES, SHRUBS, AND PERENNIALS

1. *Abelia grandiflora* 'Edward Goucher'
2. *Artemisia ludoviciana*
3. *Berberis thunbergii* 'Rose Glow'
4. *Buddleia davidii* 'Pink Delight'
5. *Caryopteris incana* 'Bluebeard'
6. *Cistus skanbergii*
7. *Cotinus coggygria* 'Royal Purple'
8. *Helichrysum angustifolium*
9. *Helleborus niger*
10. *Knautia macedonia*
11. *Lavandula angustifolia*
12. *Rosa glauca*
13. *Senecio greyii*

UNDERPLANTINGS RUNNING ALL THROUGH THE BED

Ajuga 'Burgundy Lace'

Fragaria chiloensis

Iberis

Origanum spp.

Salvia officianalis 'Tricolor'

Scilla

Silene schafta

Thymus spp.

8

ROSES IN THE
NORTHWEST GARDEN

I F ONE FLOWER EPITOMIZES romance and luxury, it's the rose, with its luscious colors, delicately cupped or ruffled petals, and heady scents. Ancient Egyptian and Chinese gardeners, monks in medieval Europe's monasteries, and even

Napoleon's empress, Josephine, fell under the spell of these delectable blooms. Over the centuries, their efforts at propagating, selecting, and hybridizing roses—along with similar efforts by countless other gardeners, famous or obscure—have resulted in the introduction of thousands of varieties of species and hybrid roses into the world's gardens.

Pacific Northwest gardeners are especially enamoured of these blooms. Portland, with its hot, sunny summers and relatively

mild winters, is a nationally renowned center for rose gardening; and even in the cooler, wetter climates of western Washington and lower British Columbia, many gardeners fill every sunny nook and cranny with roses.

Species shrubs, ramblers, and climbers were the first roses planted in gardens, with some appearing as early as 2000 B.C. in Egypt and China. By the nineteenth century, improved hybridizing techniques resulted in many varieties becoming generally available. But this development didn't always result in beautifying the garden scene—the new, comparatively skimpy and gawky hybrids that started to supplant the gloriously rambunctious old roses imposed a certain monotony onto the cultivated landscape.

Many rose lovers' gardens began to feature areas consecrated solely to hybrid roses, especially the hybrid teas. Actually, they look more like rose ghettoes, with their trussed and lopped charges standing to attention in forlorn and dreary rows, their meager leaves spotted with powdered pesticides. This approach negates the very quality of delicious prodigality that made the old roses such wonderful additions to the garden in the first place.

Today Pacific Northwesterners are seeking new ways (perhaps they are, actually, the old ways?) to plant roses in the landscape—as plants with a garden presence that extends beyond merely supporting oversized and highly colored blooms. These gardeners look for roses that have interesting foliage and attractive habits, are disease resistant, and do not require inordinate maintenance—and they want to add them to borders and beds in ways that will complement the plants surrounding them.

In other words, they want to add the roses' delicious blooms, colors, and scents to the garden's sensory mix, but not at the cost of creating still more hybrid tea ghettoes. Such gardeners find that the old varieties of species shrubs, climbers, and ramblers, as well as a new kind of hybrid shrub rose recently developed by England's David Austin, give them many of these qualities.

Consequently, these types of roses are enjoying an enormous wave of popularity among the Northwest's most dedicated rosarians—and they are helping to bring back those fabled gardens (lodged in every gardener's imagination, if not in his or her actual experience) that are rife with the roses "rich as a fig broken open, soft as a ripened peach, freckled as an apricot, coral as a pomegranate, bloomy as a bunch of grapes" conjured up by Vita Sackville-West in her introduction to Graham Stuart Thomas's *The Old Shrub Roses*.

Above: In June, Shirley and Leslie Beach's Victoria, British Columbia, garden is filled with roses and herbs.

Opposite page: Leslie Beach designed and built the arbors and trellises that support his garden's rambling and climbing roses.

Roses have a complicated family history that sometimes confuses gardeners new to them. Rosarians tell us that poring over the rose's family tree can become, in time, a consuming passion, and many books on roses explicate their lineage in painstaking detail.

This book, however, focuses primarily on the landscaping uses of roses rather than on their pedigrees. Hence, the following kinds of roses are classified according to their habits—and not, as is usual, according to their parentage—so that readers can more easily assess where to place them in their own gardens.

1. Species roses occur naturally in the wild and will reproduce truly from seed. They come in all sizes and are usually tough, vigorous, disease-resistant plants that bloom only once during the growing season. The flowers, generally cupped and with five petals, are simpler and more delicate than those of many hybrid varieties. Species roses are often good as hedges, in shrub borders, or at the backs of perennial borders.

2. Old roses are generally medium-to-large shrubby and climbing plants, often with wonderfully fragrant blooms. Blooms can be single, semidouble, or double, and most old roses bloom only once a season. With the exception of some of the China and tea roses, most old roses are quite hardy in the Pacific Northwest. They can be used for informal screening or as "room dividers" in larger gardens. Gallicas, Bourbons, albas, Chinas, damasks, teas, mosses, and hybrid perpetuals are considered old roses.

3. Climbers and ramblers are large, spreading plants that can be trained over walls, arbors, and trellises. Ramblers have flexible canes and bloom only once. Climbers have comparatively stiff canes, and some varieties are repeat bloomers.

4. Shrub roses and David Austin English roses are medium-sized plants with a variety of habits. Most of the David Austin roses are especially bred for repeat bloom, hardiness, and ease of care. They are good in shrub borders and at the backs or in the middles of perennial borders.

5. Grandifloras, polyanthas, and floribundas feature bushy habits, and repeat blooms that are often grouped in clusters or sprays. Grandifloras generally grow much taller (up to 8 feet) than polyanthas and floribundas (which generally range between 2 and 5 feet). All are good minglers in perennial beds, where their season-long blooms can act as the anchor point for color combinations involving flowers with shorter periods of bloom. Some polyanthas do well in containers.

6. Groundcovers are a small group of roses, usually growing under 2½ feet tall, that are especially useful for the front edges of perennial borders. Recommended varieties are 'Alba Meidiland', 'Max Graf', 'Magic Carpet', 'Magic Meidiland', 'The Fairy', and *Rosa paulii.*

7. Standards include many varieties of roses that can be trained as small "trees" with straight, branchless trunks that terminate in bushy heads bearing flowers. Usually standards are planted in pots, although they are sometimes planted in beds as specimens. You can add a

formal touch to any path by siting pairs of rose standards along its route. The noted rosarian David Austin suggests that the following roses train well as standards: 'Iceberg', 'Ballerina', 'Marie Louise', 'Rosa Mundi', 'Félicité Perpetué', 'Albéric Barbier', and many varieties of his English roses.

A ROMANTIC LANDSCAPE OF ROSES AND HERBS

Shirley and Leslie Beach's Garden
Victoria, British Columbia

When Shirley and Leslie Beach began their garden in 1975, they knew they wanted an "old-fashioned garden," partly because it would complement the style of their vintage Victorian cottage and partly because their taste in plants consistently runs toward the species and heirloom varieties.

Shirley says they had no grand overall plan when they began the garden. "We started out by carving a little herb garden into the big patch of lawn that originally came with the house. Then we planted a few roses in a bed near the herb garden; gradually we filled in the area between the roses and the herbs with more plants, and then the garden really was on its way."

Two factors influenced the way the Beaches' garden eventually evolved. One

A Romantic Landscape of Roses and Herbs

Shirley and Leslie Beach's Garden
Victoria, British Columbia

Garden site	*An urban garden in West Victoria, British Columbia*
Topography	*A square, mostly level lot 100 ft. on each side; the major garden area faces west*
Soil	*Heavy clay, amended with sand, mushroom compost, and household compost*
Light	*Full sun most of the day, with a few shady pockets*
Average annual rainfall	*27.7 in.*
Average minimum temperature	*37° F (2.8° C); the garden is in a wind tunnel in winter, and some tender plants that flourish in nearby gardens will die off in the Beach garden during cold snaps*
Maintenance	*Major cleanup is done in early spring, but Shirley says, "Whatever time we have, we spend in the garden" during the rest of the growing season*

Above: A thyme carpet enclosed by clipped boxwood adds formal structure to a corner of the Beaches' garden.

was the appeal that geometrically laid out planting beds have always held for both of them. "When you have some real structure in the way the garden is laid out—by using rectangular planting beds, for example—then the plants can grow any way they want to, and the garden will still have a shape and an underlying pattern," says Shirley.

Leslie has underlined their garden's formal aspects by constructing a series of wooden arbors and trellises, which divide the landscape into several distinct rooms. Rustic and cottagey in style, they add vertical definition to the garden while serving the practical function of supporting the many varieties of climbing and rambling roses trained over them.

The other major influence in the creation of the garden was Shirley's growing fascination with old roses—which are commonly defined as any class of roses, either species or hybrid, that was in existence before 1867. "I read *The Charm of Old Roses* by the New Zealander Nancy Steen, and her descriptions were so enchanting that I wanted to learn as much as I could."

Besides their beauty, the old roses have some practical qualities that will appeal to any gardener: as a class, many are hardy and disease resistant, and they generally require less pruning than many modern hybrid types. Their one great drawback is that many kinds of old roses bloom only once a year.

From the rich repertoire of this group of roses, Shirley and Leslie selected rather dense, shrubby varieties to serve as informal hedges around the perimeter of their garden, and climbers and ramblers to grow on the garden structures. Among Shirley's old rose favorites are 'Charles de Mills', a 5-foot-high gallica with a vigorous habit that has deep purple blooms swirling around a green eye ("It's sexy!"), and 'Mme. Hardy', a tall damask growing upright and thickly leaved, with many-petaled white blooms that possess a tinge of pink. Both have a delicious scent.

Among Shirley's favorite ramblers are 'Adélaide D'Orléans', which grows to 15 feet in prime conditions and features wonderfully creamy, ruffled, many-petaled blooms that hang down in clusters, and 'Veilchenblau', a vigorous scrambler (sometimes classed among the climbers) that grows 12 feet tall, with knockout crimson-violet blooms you can see a mile away.

Perennials and herbs bring color to the garden even after the first flush of roses subsides in late June.

Because none of these roses bloom recurrently, Shirley and Leslie have extended the seasonal color in their garden in several ways. First, they grow clematis on or near the old roses, either staggering the blooming period so that there is color from the clematis blooms before or after the rose flush, or coordinating the bloom times so that the rose and clematis flowers will play off each other. Shirley notes that roses and clematis combine particularly well "because they need similar growing conditions." Rose and clematis color combinations she finds especially appealing are the soft pink blooms of the rambler 'Mme. Sancy de Parabère' threaded with the mauvy-purple flowers of *Clematis* 'Mrs. P. T. James', and the apricot-pink blooms of *R.* 'Buff Beauty' twined with the clustering, double-petaled violet flowers of *C. viticella* 'Purpurea Plena Elegans'.

The Beaches also underplant their roses with violets, pansies, auricula primroses, "and lots of gray plants," including lamb's-ears *(Stachys lanata,* also known as *Stachy byzantina),* artemisias, lavender cottons *(Santolina chamae-cyparissus),* and campanulas. Because most of their old rose varieties have purple or pink flowers, they tend to confine their color scheme for the blooms of the underplantings to whites, lavenders, and blues. "We use very little in the way of orange or harsh red in the garden," Shirley says, because they find these colors difficult to blend into the predominant color scheme.

There is something appealingly timeless about the garden Shirley and Leslie Beach have created around their Victoria cottage. Perhaps it's because it is filled with roses and herbs—which are, after all, some of the very earliest plants that humans domesticated for use in their gardens, and which consequently have the delicious allure of tradition and lore attached to them. Or perhaps it's the sheer romantic glamour of the mingled roses, clematis, herbs, and flowering perennials. Whatever the reason, visitors happily while away sunny afternoons here, almost intoxicated by the luscious fragrances and ruffly clouds of petals, almost hypnotized by the sound of bees softly bumbling in the blooms.

❀ ROSEHIPS AND BIRDHOUSES
Margaret Willoughby's Garden
Portland, Oregon

Margaret Willoughby's twin passions are roses and birds, and her Portland garden creates a haven for both. Margaret grew up on a 9000-acre farm in Australia, where she played in her grandmother's spacious rose garden as a child. "*Everybody gardens where I grew up, it's something that everybody just knows how to do,*" she recalls.

This sense of gardening as an entirely natural, almost instinctive, human activity has influenced the way Margaret created her garden. It almost seems alive—like an organism that carries on a complicated and beautifully integrated existence of its own—one in which Margaret plays an active, collaborative, but not dominating, role.

"Seems" is the operative word here, of course, since the garden possesses this apparently spontaneous and unstudied charm due chiefly to Margaret's ingenious approach to design.

Roses, especially old shrub, rambling, and climbing roses, form the green architecture of the garden. Planted in naturally arranged clusters, they create informal hedges between the various rooms, mark points of entry and exit, and act as transitions from one planting area to another.

Among Margaret's favorite roses to use as room

Rosehips and Birdhouses	
Margaret Willoughby's Garden	
Portland, Oregon	
GARDEN SITE	*An urban cottage garden near downtown Portland*
TOPOGRAPHY	*A level lot 125 ft. long by 69 ft. wide, on top of a small hill; the house is almost in the middle of the garden*
SOIL	*Heavy clay, leavened with mushroom compost, sand, and fine gravel*
LIGHT	*The south-facing back garden and the west-facing side garden are mostly sunny; the north-facing front garden and east-facing side garden are in dappled shade*
AVERAGE ANNUAL RAINFALL	*39.4 in.*
AVERAGE MINIMUM TEMPERATURE	*39° F (3.9° C); a very cold east wind whistles down the street in winter*
MAINTENANCE	*Margaret doesn't keep track of time spent working in the garden because "it's all fun, I don't think of it as work"*

dividers is 'Constance Spry', a David Austin English rose that grows to 7 feet or taller, with a sprawling habit that makes it seem much larger. Margaret says 'Constance' will take a lot of pruning and still come back with a magnificent "blowsy" look that she adores. The blooms (they occur only once each growing season) are theatrically large and ruffled, warmly pink, and exceptionally fragrant. 'Constance' also trains well against a wall or over an arbor.

'Cerise Bouquet' is another sprawling shrub rose, growing to the enormous size of 15 feet tall and 15 feet wide in Margaret's garden. It features arching canes, along whose tops hang delicate clusters of deep cerise-pink flowers. It has a rich fragrance but also blooms only once in the growing season.

A climber that Margaret uses in a sunny shrub border, 'Mme. Grégoire Staechelin', has a shrubby habit, attractive shiny leaves, and large ruffled blooms with both dark and light pink petals. Margaret says she especially enjoys looking up into the face of this rose, whose fragrance "is heavenly."

Along the east side of the house, Margaret established a narrow, leafy tunnel of rugosas, gallicas, and hybrid groundcovers that will bloom in dappled shade. She particularly recommends 'Complicata', an arching gallica 12 feet tall with large, deep pink blooms with yellow stamens, 'Agnes', a rugosa hybrid with fragrant, pale yellow, repeat flowers, and 'Marjorie Fair', a short shrub rose often used as a groundcover, with clusters of cherry red flowers that bloom almost continuously.

Margaret trains climbers and ramblers over arbors in the back garden, but she also twines roses through trees so that they are able to achieve their maximum height. 'Rambling Rector' is a dense and bushy rambler that cloaks a fruit tree with a magnificent profusion of small, creamy-white blooms in June. The fragrant, deep gold blooms of a pioneer rose, 'Harison's Yellow', clamber through the foliage of a group of shrubs planted in dappled shade.

Birds find a welcome in this rose garden year-round, where they can nest and forage in tall thickets, dine on

Above: Margaret Willoughby's garden, ten minutes from downtown Portland, is a haven for roses and birds.

Left: Arbors, trellises, and brick paths edge a formal stretch of lawn in Margaret's back garden. Tall shrub roses help to make a "green wall" between this area and the rest of the garden.

choice aphids and slugs in summer, and pick over nutritious rosehips left on the branches in winter. Margaret also makes sure there is always running water available for them, and weaves garlands of seeds that she hangs in the trees when rosehips become sparse in late winter.

The tradition of planting roses in geometric beds amidst formal hardscapes remains strong in the Northwest, but gardens such as Margaret Willoughby's show us how roses can find an entirely natural place in an informally planted regional garden as well.

CHECKLIST FOR PLANTING ROSES

- Rose growers recommend a sunny spot with good air circulation for growing roses. The soil should be rich in humus and water-retentive. (However, Shirley Beach finds her old roses take to the rather heavy clay soil of her garden quite well—she does no special amending when she plants them.)

- Try to buy roses that are grown on their own rootstocks; even if their canes die back in a bad freeze, the new growth will come true from the roots. A rose grafted onto a different rootstock will under the same circumstances revert to the original rose. (Margaret Willoughby buys only roses grown on their own rootstocks from nurseries located north of Portland, where she lives. Margaret finds that roses grown in California and other points south are often too tender for her garden.)

- Old folk sayings tell us not to plant roses in spots where roses have previously grown because the ground will become "rose sick" and the new plants will fail to thrive. Whatever the reasons for this phenomenon—and there is some evidence that toxins cast from the roots of the earlier rose may affect the new plant—many rosarians suggest you plant roses in "virgin" soil.

- Plant roses either in fall (mulching them well) or in spring once the ground has warmed.

- The classic advice for planting a bare-root rose runs as follows: dig a hole 2 feet wide by 2 feet deep, mix a bag of steer manure into the soil at the bottom of the hole, fashion a mound of dirt at the bottom of the hole, and gently spread the roots over the mound. (Make sure the rose graft, if any, is above ground level when you start to fill in the soil around the plant.) Fill in the rest of the hole with topsoil, pressing it down gently to eliminate air pockets. Form a little ridge of dirt around the hole so that water will run toward the plant rather than away from it. Water the plant thoroughly, and then mulch it with 2 to 3 inches of compost (many rosarians use mushroom compost), keeping the mulch well away from the stem of the plant.

- Water roses with soaker hoses or with hand-held hoses directed at the roots. Overhead watering can damage blooms as well as promote disease on the wet foliage.

- Don't feed roses for the purpose of stimulating blooms during the first year; instead, let all the energy go to the roots so that the plant can establish itself quickly and vigorously. (This means you should use fertilizers specifically formulated to encourage root growth, ones that are high in potash and potassium.)

  Once you are fertilizing for bloom, Margaret Willoughby suggests you avoid the new systemic rose fertilizers, which often contain toxic elements that remain in the treated soil for as long as five years. She suggests an alternative program of building up your roses through a year-round cycle of mulching with rich composts, and of spraying rose leaves once a month during the growing season with 1 tablespoon of fish fertilizer dissolved in 1 gallon of water.

- Mildew and black spot plague Northwest rose gardens, but here are several alternatives to spraying your roses with chemicals—which can be harmful to the environment, wildlife, your pets, and you:

  Acquire roses that resist disease (many nurseries now provide this kind of information).

  Examine your plants often—try to catch a problem early, before it gets a widespread grip in the garden. Early control measures include picking off diseased leaves and casting them in the trash (not the compost bin!). Don't allow affected leaves to lie on the

Above: Rosa *'Eden', a large-flowered climber, weaves through a trellis in the Portland, Oregon, garden of Wayne Hughes and Danny Hills.*

Right: The large white-blooming rambler 'Bobby James' climbs over a picket fence in the Hughes-Hills garden. R. 'William Baffin' (lower left) is a new shrub rose that withstands Portland winters well.

Opposite page: The large white flowers of the rambler 'Dr. W. Van Fleet' almost engulf a birdhouse in Margaret Willoughby's garden. On the right is the ancient 'Apothecary's Rose' (R. gallica officinalis), *a fragrant old rose with pink blooms.*

NORTHWEST GARDENERS' FAVORITE ROSES

Many of the gardeners presented in previous chapters are also dedicated rose growers; the following lists include their favorite varieties, along with their comments on each rose's characteristics and growing habits.

LARRY FEENEY'S FAVORITE ROSES

'Gloire de Dijon'	"An old rose that has been hardy for me with good mulching for winter. Trained as a climber, a beautiful buffy-pink, many-petaled and voluptuous. Lovely scent as well." Grows to 5 feet.
'Hume's Blush Tea'	"This is my current love-affair (a 3-inch start is being nurtured in my greenhouse over the winter). What is incredible here is the *scent*—just like guava and gloriously fragrant. The color is off-white/lemon/blush pink, if you know what I mean." Larry has hopes this China tea will flourish in a sheltered spot in his garden, despite its reputation for tenderness in our region.
'Mme. Hardy'	"A popular and vigorous damask that blooms only once a year but quite prolifically and over an extended spell. Pure white with a distinctive green eye ('the green-eyed temptress'). Lots of blossoms, and she climbed more than 20 feet into our laurel hedge! Most specimens I've seen are rather more well disciplined."
'Emanuel'	A David Austin shrub rose growing to 4 feet. "Not a prolific bloomer for me, but the color—a wonderfully subtle apricot-pink—is a knockout. We are now learning that the David Austins can be quite hardy."
Rosa sericea	"Simple white flowers, but growing on incredible red stems with huge, translucent, rampant thorns that literally make people gasp. A vigorous grower that needs cutting back to keep in bounds and to encourage the breathtaking new growth." A species rose growing to 10 feet.
Rosa moyesii	"Various types, most with red, yellow-stamened flowers. A big bush, but the main attraction are the hips—profuse red-orange flagon-shaped clusters. Mine has just finished its first year (and no hips yet), but I have great hopes. Last year's heart-throb. I must learn patience."

MARGARET LOCKETT'S FAVORITE ROSES

'Heritage'	A David Austin English shrub rose growing to 5 feet. David Austin himself calls 'Heritage' "perhaps the most beautiful English rose," noting its blush-pink color, shell-delicate petals, shrubby foliage, and strong fragrance.
'Graham Stuart Thomas'	An early David Austin English rose growing to 5 feet. A gloriously profuse first flush of satiny, deep yellow blooms touched with apricot is succeeded by several more flushes later in the summer,
'Sombreuil'	A hardy climbing tea growing to 10 feet, with ruffled cream blooms that repeat well into fall; a wonderful scent.

NORTHWEST GARDENERS' FAVORITE ROSES (cont.)

MARGARET LOCKETT'S FAVORITE ROSES (cont.)

'French Lace'
A low-growing (2½- to 3-foot) floribunda with creamy white repeating blooms; a good mixer in the perennial border.

'Golden Wings'
A shrub rose growing to 5 feet, with pearly-gold single blooms with apricot stamens; the repeat blooms glow deliciously against the purple-ash foliage of *Sambucus nigra*.

SARAH PEARL'S FAVORITE ROSES

'Dortmund'
A climber growing to 8 feet, with single "bright red blooms shading to white in the center that go well with pink" in flower combinations; easy-care and disease resistant, a repeat bloomer.

'Buff Beauty'
A hybrid musk shrub rose growing to 5 feet, with "attractive foliage and repeat apricot-pink blooms that look good with purples; easy-care and disease resistant."

'Margo Koster'
A dwarf Polyantha with "salmony-orange blooms that grows well in containers. We leave our Margo Kosters outside in their 18" by 18" containers during the winter after setting them near a protected wall and mulching them. They are virtually thornless, easy-care roses." A repeat bloomer.

'Iceberg'
A freely flowering floribunda (often classed as a shrub rose) growing to 4 feet, with pure white, repeating blooms. "We have an 'Iceberg' standard that stays outside in winter after we put loose insulation over the trunk's two graft points and mulch the plant's roots. I prune the standard's top every year or two to promote blooms. 'Iceberg' can take some high shade in my garden."

'The Fairy'
A perpetual shrub rose (sometimes classed with the polyanthas) growing to 3 feet, with clusters of ruffled pink flowers "that bloom almost continuously. We use them both as standards and as shrubs."

'Paul's Himalayan Musk'
"A vigorous rambler we are growing up into an ornamental cherry tree." The supple canes support sprays of small pink blooms that David Austin likens to cherry blossoms. "It only blooms once, but is so beautiful it's worth having anyway."

PAMELA GEORGES'S FAVORITE ROSES

'Morning Jewel'
A climbing floribunda growing to 8 feet. "My all-time favorite rose, because the hot-pink blooms begin in June and keep going past frost. It has beautiful hips and always stays vigorous and healthy."

'Lucetta'
A David Austin English shrub rose that grows "like a climber" to 5 feet. "A nonstop show all summer, and it has gorgeous ruffly pink petals with apricot tinges."

NORTHWEST GARDENERS' FAVORITE ROSES (cont.)

PAMELA GEORGES'S FAVORITE ROSES (cont.)

'Belle Story'
A David Austin English shrub rose growing to 4 feet. "Belle has really nice foliage, it's a repeat bloomer, and the flowers—delicate pink semidoubles—don't show rain damage."

'Pleasure'
A floribunda growing to 3 feet. "This is a great rose for a small garden. Its ruffled coral-pink blooms look good in almost any color combination with other plants. The beautiful foliage has a sort of ruffly wave in the leaves."

'Magic Carpet'
A groundcover rose growing 2 feet high and 4 feet wide. A bright, full-bodied red "that looks wonderful mixed in with snow-in-summer *(Cerastium tomentosum).*"

Below: R. 'Rambling Rector' (right), a giant shrub rose with small, free-flowering white blooms, in Margaret Willoughby's garden.
Opposite page: R. 'Prioress' (lower right) flourishes under high shade in the Bainbridge Island, Washington, garden of Lindsay Smith.

ground underneath the plant, because the disease can spread from the discarded leaves to the plant.

Birds eat aphids and slugs, so attract them to your garden by providing year-round moving water and some plants that bear berries, rosehips, and seeds. (See Chapter Two for plant lists.)

Margaret Willoughby reports that when she visited Christopher Lloyd's famous gardens at Great Dixter in Suffolk, the gardeners were spreading lawn clippings around the bases of the shrubs. They explained they were working under the theory that when the clippings heat up under the summer sun, they will kill bacteria lurking in the soil beneath them.

Ladybugs (which can be purchased by the thousands in little net bags at nurseries) can be highly effective in controlling aphids. I had three *Rosa rugosa* shrubs so overwhelmed with aphids during two growing seasons that hosing them off several times a day, and even spraying them with Orthene, simply didn't work. I was ready to uproot them and leave the patch of soil bare for a year, but fortunately decided, as a last expedient, to open a package of hungry ladybugs at their base one still evening instead. The next morning not a single aphid remained, and the roses continue to flourish, without aphids, three years later!

For a nontoxic treatment for black spot, Margaret Willoughby recommends dissolving 1 tablespoon of bicarbonate of soda in 1 gallon of water and spraying the affected areas.

If mildew, black spot, and/or aphids have gained such a serious grip on your roses that ultimate measures must be taken, Margaret suggests that 1 tablespoon of Funginex (for mildew and black spot) and 1 tablespoon of Orthene (for aphids), dissolved together in 1 gallon of water and sprayed onto the affected leaves, should solve the problem. Treat monthly.

• Many regional rose growers advise that you go easy on pruning roses, especially varieties of old roses, climbers, ramblers, and David Austin English roses. (Shirley Beach says she prunes her roses *only* in order to control their growth over pathways; other regional growers suggest leaving new plants unpruned for their first two or three years at a minimum.)

- Prune in late February (earlier pruning may stimulate premature growth, which can be harmed later if the weather turns cold again).
- When deadheading old blooms to stimulate new growth, cut the rose stem back to the next five-leaved stem, angling the cut in the direction in which you would like the new growth to grow.

ROSES FOR SPECIAL PURPOSES

Several thousand varieties of roses are available to the home gardener, and often the beginner doesn't know where to start. Because there are so many options, you can afford to choose only the very best varieties that suit your purposes. Of course, it's in the cards that at some point you will lose your heart to some fair unknown, whose strengths and weaknesses you will discover only after it is planted in your garden. If you decide to take such a chance, then bravo and good luck!—since chance-taking is one of the fundamental factors in learning how to garden with style.

Below are rose varieties, many of which have been mentioned in this chapter, that regional gardeners recommend for specific characteristics.

ROSES FOR SPECIAL PURPOSES	
Attractive foliage	'Belle Story', 'Buff Beauty', 'Cerise Bouquet', 'Pleasure', *Rosa glauca, Rosa hugonis, Rosa rugosa*
Disease resistance	'Agnes', 'Bonica', 'Buff Beauty', 'Charles de Mills', 'Complicata', 'Constance Spry', 'Dortmund', 'The Fairy', 'French Lace', 'Harison's Yellow', 'Mme. Hardy', 'Morning Jewel', and most species roses
Waterwise	'Buff Beauty', 'Dortmund', 'La Sevillana', 'The Fairy', 'Fimbriata', 'Frühlingsgold', 'Pretty Jessica', *Rosa eglanteria, Rosa glauca, Rosa rugosa,* and many groundcover roses
Shade tolerance	'Agnes', albas, 'Cerise Bouquet', 'Complicata', 'Harison's Yellow', 'Iceberg', 'Marjorie Fair', 'Pax', 'Scarlet Meidiland'

INDEX

(Page numbers in boldface indicate illustrations or plant list.)